THE LIFE HISTORY OF THE UNITED STATES

Volume 12: From 1945

THE GREAT AGE OF CHANGE

THE LIFE HISTORY OF THE UNITED STATES

THE **LIFE** HISTORY OF THE UNITED STATES

Consulting Editor, Henry F. Graff

Volume 12: From 1945

THE GREAT AGE OF CHANGE

by William E. Leuchtenburg

and the Editors of LIFE

TIME INCORPORATED, NEW YORK
A STONEHENGE BOOK

THE AUTHOR of Volumes 11 and 12 of this series, William E. Leuchtenburg, has concentrated on the study of the United States during the 20th Century. At present Professor of American History at Columbia University, he has taught at Smith College, New York University and Harvard. During the summer of 1956 Dr. Leuchtenburg lectured at the Salzburg Seminar for American Studies in Austria, and in 1961-1962 he was a Fellow at the Center for Advanced Study in the Behavioral Sciences, Stanford, California. He is the author of *The Perils of Prosperity, 1914-1932*, and won the 1964 Bancroft Prize for *Franklin D. Roosevelt and the New Deal, 1932-1940*.

THE CONSULTING EDITOR for this series, Henry F. Graff, is Chairman of the Department of History at Columbia University.

TIME-LIFE BOOKS

EDITOR *Norman P. Ross*
TEXT DIRECTOR *William Jay Gold* ART DIRECTOR *Edward A. Hamilton*
CHIEF OF RESEARCH *Beatrice T. Dobie*

Editorial staff for Volume 12,
THE LIFE HISTORY OF THE UNITED STATES

SERIES EDITOR *Sam Welles*
ASSISTANT EDITOR *Jerry Korn*
DESIGNER *Frank Crump*
STAFF WRITERS *Peter Meyerson, Gerald Simons, Timothy Carr*
CHIEF RESEARCHER *Clara E. Nicolai*
RESEARCHERS *Mary Youatt, Patricia Tolles, Ruth Silva, Mary-Jo Kline, Terry Drucker, Ellen Leiman, Elizabeth Collins, Malabar Brodeur, Jacqueline Coates, Martha Brean*
PICTURE RESEARCHERS *Margaret K. Goldsmith, Theo Pascal*
ART ASSOCIATE *Robert L. Young*
ART ASSISTANTS *James D. Smith, Wayne R. Young, Douglas B. Graham*
COPY STAFF *Marian Gordon Goldman, Gail Weesner, Dolores A. Littles*

PUBLISHER *Rhett Austell*
GENERAL MANAGER *John A. Watters*

LIFE MAGAZINE

EDITOR
Edward K. Thompson

MANAGING EDITOR
George P. Hunt

PUBLISHER
Jerome S. Hardy

Valuable assistance in the preparation of this volume was given by Roger Butterfield, who served as picture consultant; Michael Rougier and Paul Schutzer, LIFE staff photographers; Doris O'Neil, Chief of the LIFE Picture Library; Richard M. Clurman, Chief of the TIME-LIFE News Service; and Content Peckham, Chief of the Time Inc. Bureau of Editorial Reference.

THE COVER shows astronaut John Glenn soaring into his nation's history by—in his words—"hitting a keyhole in the sky" as the first American to orbit the earth. This is a detail of the picture which appears on pages 124-125.

CONTENTS

1. COLD WAR

On a sunny Wednesday afternoon in late June 1945 the *Queen Mary*, carrying more than 14,500 veterans of the war in Europe, steamed into New York harbor. As word went out that the first large shipment of soldiers was arriving from the fighting fronts, harbor whistles screeched their greeting, and ferryboats, rust-caked old freighters, baby flattops—all the craft of the river —turned out to bid it welcome. The boys were on their way home. By late August, after the fall of Japan, they were beginning to arrive back from every part of the globe.

They returned to a world where much seemed the same. The country was whistling the same kind of songs, showing the same kind of movies. Nothing could have been more reassuring. The veterans wanted above all to put the strife of the world behind them and pick up the broken ends of their lives.

The war had been fought with few illusions, and there was little expectation that the postwar years would be utopian. Yet it did seem that a secure peace had been won and that a long era free from the demands of war now lay ahead. To be sure, there was already some uneasiness over Russian actions, but since it seemed certain that the U.S.S.R. would take years to recover from the devastation of the war, and since America held a monopoly on the atomic bomb which the Soviet Union was not likely to break for many years to come, there was little cause for alarm.

Besides, most Americans thought it would be simple to get on with the

A MONUMENT TO PEACE, the United Nations Building juts into the Manhattan dusk. Truman called the U.N. Charter an avowal of "faith that war is not inevitable."

Russians. As Franklin D. Roosevelt had put it during the war, the Russians might not be "housebroken," but they were nevertheless "a very good breed of dog." On his return from a trip to Moscow in late 1945, General Dwight D. Eisenhower concluded that "nothing guides Russian policy so much as a desire for friendship with the United States."

Few men in 1945 foresaw how swiftly these expectations would be shattered. When the *Queen Mary* was nudged into its berth in the North River, no one had yet heard the words "Cold War" or "Iron Curtain." In less than two years they would be on everyone's lips. In less than three years the two great wartime allies would be on the brink of war in Berlin. In little more than four years the White House would summon newsmen to announce that Soviet Russia had exploded an atomic device. Thereafter either power could trigger a world war that would devastate both countries and leave much, perhaps all, of the world uninhabitable.

To guide the American people in this treacherous new world, fate had singled out a man who was, like the people themselves, untested. On April 12, 1945, Vice President Harry S. Truman, after a day of presiding over a dull Senate debate, was summoned to the White House. When he reached the executive mansion, Mrs. Roosevelt came forward, put her arm about his shoulder and said: "Harry, the President is dead." Stunned, Truman finally managed to blurt out: "Is there anything I can do for you?" She responded: "Is there anything *we* can do for *you*? For you are the one in trouble now."

Herbert Agar later wrote: "During the next few years this strange little man—lively and pert to the verge of bumptiousness; more widely read in history than any President since John Quincy Adams; more wilful than any President since James K. Polk; more incompetent in dividing the good from the bad among his own friends at home than any President since Warren Harding—would make and enforce a series of decisions upon which, for better or for worse, our world now rests, or shakes."

Truman greeted his elevation to the highest office in the land as if it were a cruel trick of the gods. "Boys, if you ever pray, pray for me now," he told reporters. "I don't know whether you fellows ever had a load of hay fall on you. But when they told me yesterday what had happened I felt like the moon, the stars and all the planets had fallen on me."

Shriner, Eagle, member of the Baptist Church, Harry Truman of Independence, Missouri, had a hard time realizing he was President of the United States of America. On his first full day in the office, he went up to Capitol Hill to have lunch with his friends in the Senate as he always had. He started to walk onto the Senate floor, but the Secretary of the Senate, Leslie Biffle, stopped him: "You can't go out there, Harry, you are the President now!" Truman turned unhappily away.

No presidential transition is ever easy, but this particular one could not have come at a worse time. The grand alliance between the U.S.S.R. and the West was beginning to disintegrate as Russian commissars, in violation of agreements, snuffed out the independence of Eastern European countries. Truman confessed that he was not particularly well informed on foreign policy. He had not been privy to the negotiations at Yalta or the details of vexing issues like the Polish boundaries. Night after night he sat up late poring over State Department documents in the effort to bring himself up to date.

Commemorating America's post-war aid to Greece under the Truman Doctrine, a huge statue of President Harry S. Truman is installed in a square in Athens. The figure was attacked as a work of art, and Truman himself doubted the wisdom of erecting a statue of a living person. "You never know," he said, "when you have to turn around and tear it down."

To complicate matters, neither Secretary of State Edward Stettinius Jr. nor James F. Byrnes, who succeeded him in July 1945, had any special competence in foreign affairs. Winston Churchill later noted the "deadly hiatus which existed between the fading of President Roosevelt's strength and the growth of President Truman's grip of the vast world problems."

Truman's first steps were not reassuring. In his fourth week in office he signed, without even reading it, an order which precipitately halted the delivery of lend-lease goods. The abrupt termination of the program caused not only hardship but acute resentment among America's allies, especially Russia. Truman later wrote: "That experience brought home to me not only that I had to know exactly where I was going but also that I had to know that my basic policies were being carried out. If I had read the order, as I should have, the incident would not have occurred." Lend-lease was resumed, but the damage had been done. Some of the blame for breaking up the grand alliance had to be borne by the United States.

Truman also revealed in his first days in office that he had little patience with Soviet tergiversations. When Russian Foreign Minister V. M. Molotov attempted to explain away the U.S.S.R.'s failure to honor its pledges with respect to Poland, Truman gave him a dressing down. "I have never been talked to like that in my life," Molotov exclaimed. "Carry out your agreements," Truman snapped, "and you won't get talked to like that!"

YET Truman also had a profound faith in the possibilities of a world organization to preserve the peace. In the summer and fall of 1944 at the Dumbarton Oaks estate in Washington, D.C., the major powers had worked out a tentative sketch of a new international organization; this was to be presented to delegates at a conference scheduled for San Francisco in April 1945. Truman's first decision was that the San Francisco Conference was not to be postponed because of Roosevelt's death but would meet on schedule.

Foreign leaders had been delighted by America's willingness to sponsor the world conference, but during the planning period they still feared that Republican isolationists such as Senator Arthur Vandenberg of Michigan would block American commitment to an international organization, just as Henry Cabot Lodge and his supporters had in 1920. Vandenberg had voted against repeal of the arms embargo, against the Selective Service bill, against lend-lease. When the lend-lease bill was adopted in 1941, the Michigan senator had noted in his diary: "If America 'cracks up' you can put your finger on this precise moment as the time when the crime was committed."

But the war shook Vandenberg's confidence in America's ability to isolate itself from the rest of the world. On January 10, 1945, before an astonished and raptly attentive Senate, he abandoned isolationism. "I do not believe," he said, "that any nation hereafter can immunize itself by its own exclusive action." American newspapers hailed Vandenberg's "conversion." One writer noted: "In an old-fashioned revival meeting, the conversion of an ordinary citizen stirs only perfunctory hosannas. But when a notorious, grizzled old sinner hits the sawdust trail, the hallelujahs shake the tabernacle." Quick to take advantage of Vandenberg's change of heart, President Roosevelt invited him to be a delegate to the forthcoming San Francisco Conference.

On April 25, 1945, the day American and Soviet troops embraced on the Elbe, the conference opened in San Francisco's Opera House. For the next

Home from the war in Europe, two GIs aboard the "Queen Mary" celebrate as the ship docks in New York in July 1945. Those veterans returning with long combat records were sent to separation centers and quickly discharged. Many others, reassigned to finish the war against Japan, complained bitterly. But the fighting was over before many of them even arrived.

9

nine weeks, while the war in the Pacific was still being waged, 800 delegates debated the shape of the world that would emerge from the fighting.

The main design of the new organization had already been drawn by the big powers at Dumbarton Oaks. Each member nation would be represented in a General Assembly, but the real authority would reside in an 11-member Security Council in which the United States, Britain, Russia, France and China would have permanent seats. A permanent member could veto any move to impose sanctions against it. The time would come when the veto would seem to be a Soviet invention: By 1962 the U.S.S.R. would have used it 100 times, the United States not once. But the fact is that no nation insisted more strongly on the right to the veto than the United States.

In addition to the Security Council and the General Assembly and an International Court of Justice, there were to be subsidiary agencies: an Economic and Social Council, a Secretariat, a Trusteeship Council, among others. At the Bretton Woods Conference in 1944, the International Bank for Reconstruction and Development and the International Monetary Fund had been created to stimulate and stabilize the world's economies. In November 1943 the United Nations Relief and Rehabilitation Administration had been set up; most of UNRRA's campaign to bring relief to war-ravaged areas was financed by the United States, and two Americans, Herbert Lehman and Fiorello La Guardia, successively held the top administrative post in the agency.

While the Soviet Union came out of the San Francisco Conference with only minimal concessions, the United States won a charter that embodied all the major objectives it sought. In particular, it achieved the substance of its desire to preserve the Pan-American system and to handle the colonial question in a fashion that would not prejudice its future control of Japanese-mandated islands in the Pacific.

Soviet intransigence on one minor procedural question almost wrecked the conference. Molotov insisted that a permanent member should be empowered to use the veto even to prevent any discussion of a complaint directed against the member. As the conference foundered, Harry Hopkins, critically ill, pleaded with Stalin to reverse his envoy. When Stalin agreed to accept the American interpretation, the last roadblock was removed. At noon on June 26, 1945, the delegates filed in to the Veterans' Building in San Francisco to affix their names to the Charter of the United Nations.

The United States had played a major role in creating the new postwar organization. But the United States had played such a role before, and then, when the treaty had come before the Senate, it had been rejected. All through the months of negotiation, the world had wondered anxiously whether the unhappy experience of the League of Nations would be repeated. Such fears were groundless. A month after the signing of the charter, the Senate approved it 89-2. The United States was the first major power to ratify.

B<small>UT</small> devotion to world co-operation was hardly enough. The United States had to be willing to mobilize sufficient military force to discourage the Soviet Union from actions that would jeopardize the peace. Eventually America would learn this lesson so well that it would lay itself open to the criticism that it was relying almost wholly on military power. But in the immediate aftermath of the war, America had yet to learn the simplest lessons of power politics. The United States, indeed, extended a wide-open invitation to the

Patrician F.D.R.'s intimate friend and adviser was Harry Hopkins, son of an Iowa harness maker. When Roosevelt died and Truman took over, Hopkins went to Moscow and got Stalin to reverse a stand that threatened the U.N. talks at San Francisco. Truman said Hopkins saved the conference.

U.S. Senator, Supreme Court Justice and Secretary of State, James Byrnes was a tough-minded pragmatist. He was known above all else as a man who got things done. A cab driver, analyzing Byrnes's success, said, "That's his specialty—getting people to say yes to things that they want to say no to."

Russians to expand their sphere by pulling its own troops out of Europe and the Orient at breakneck speed. Of the eight million men in the Army on V-J Day, only 4.3 million were left at the end of the year.

Even this pell-mell demobilization was not fast enough for war-weary veterans. On January 4, 1946, the War Department announced that it would be necessary to slow up discharges and modify the discharge system in order to retain some essential men. GIs overseas touched off a series of angry protests. Riots started in Manila, where 2,500 soldiers marched on the headquarters of the commanding general, and quickly spread to Hawaii, Guam, Germany, Britain and other points. In Washington General Eisenhower was ambushed by irate women representing "Bring Back Daddy" clubs. The experience, Ike said, left him "emotionally upset." By the summer of 1946, the Army had been reduced to 1.5 million men; the Navy to 700,000.

Arthur Vandenberg, preparing for a meeting with European statesmen, decided to learn Russian. In listening to Foreign Minister Molotov talking to an interpreter, he asked what a phrase he had heard meant. "You don't need to know the phrase 'Ya soglasen,'" replied Molotov, ". . . it means 'I agree.'"

BY this time the West was beginning to learn some of the hard facts of military power. In the spring of 1945 Russian armies had overrun Eastern Europe, and the Kremlin, its military authority supreme, left no doubt that it would prevent the creation of autonomous, democratic governments there. At an Anglo-American-Russian meeting held in the summer of 1945 at Potsdam, Stalin had explained bluntly that in Eastern Europe any "freely elected government would be anti-Soviet and that we cannot allow." Powerless to reverse the Soviet policies, the Allies had to acquiesce in them.

The drafting of peace treaties with the minor Axis powers had been left to an Allied Council of Foreign Ministers. Its sessions, held from September 1945 to December 1946 in London, Paris and New York, made it clear that the wartime unity with the Soviet Union could not be maintained. The parleys were interminable and futile. Senator Tom Connally, who participated in these meetings, said, "All you do is sit all day going yah, yah, yah."

But that was just a sideshow; the fundamental test of unity among the big powers was Germany. Each of the four occupying powers—America, Britain, Russia and France—was to administer its own zone in the defeated nation, but all were to participate in an Allied Control Council responsible for Germany as a whole. Germany was a land neither side possessed, the testing ground of whether East and West could learn to live with one another.

When Harold Stassen joined the Navy, many thought him just another glory-seeking politician. But he became an object of veneration as a good luck omen. Even after the costly fighting at Bougainville and Manila, his ships were only slightly damaged. "They used to rub me for luck," Stassen recalled.

The United States, at the outset, was less troubled by possible disagreement with the U.S.S.R. than with making sure that Germany never again gave birth to a monstrous regime like that of Nazism. In the closing weeks of the war, American troops had discovered the full horror of Hitler's Germany—the concentration camps, the gas chambers, the instruments of death and torture which had been used to exterminate millions of Jews and other victims of the Nazis. The United States was determined to punish the perpetrators of these deeds. It joined with the Russians, British and French to create an International Military Tribunal before which 22 high German officials were tried between November 1945 and October 1946.

Into the courtroom on the opening day of the Nuremberg trials filed the prisoners: Reich Marshal Hermann Goering, fat and restless in his pearl-gray uniform; the blank-faced, listless Rudolf Hess, feigning amnesia; Hans Frank, the brutal governor of Poland; Holland's gauleiter Arthur Seyss-Inquart; the Jew-baiting Julius Streicher; military leaders including Field Marshal Wilhelm Keitel; civilian functionaries led by Hjalmar Schacht. On November

29, 1945, the courtroom darkened, and for 52 minutes films of the concentration camps were shown. Goering's face reddened, Keitel mopped his brow, Schacht refused to look at the screen ("No! I'll get sick," he cried).

On October 1, 1946, the court found 19 of the accused guilty; three, among them Schacht, were acquitted. Twelve—including Hitler's missing lieutenant Martin Bormann, tried *in absentia*—were sentenced to die. The unregenerate Goering escaped the noose by committing suicide on October 15. The following day the remaining 10 were hanged.

Some people were troubled by the doubtful legal basis for the trials, which, as Churchill stated, created the dangerous precedent that "the leaders of a nation defeated in war shall be put to death by the victors." Yet none of the critics advanced a proposal that met the widely felt need to punish those responsible for such terrible crimes. "Either the victors must judge the vanquished," said American prosecutor Robert Jackson as the trials started, "or we must leave the defeated to judge themselves."

THE United States began its occupation of its zone of Germany with a tough policy. American troops were forbidden to "fraternize" with Germans. To erase Germany's war potential, steel and chemical production were curbed and cartels disbanded.

But as friction with Russia over occupation policies increased, the United States began to modify its attitude toward Germany. At Potsdam the powers had agreed that each country was to take reparations from its own zone; since the Russian zone was more agrarian, the Western powers would ship 15 per cent of the capital equipment in their zones to the U.S.S.R. in return for food, coal and other raw materials. However, the Russians were not only stripping their zone of factories but, contrary to the agreement, were taking goods from current production. Such a policy could lead only to chaos or, as the Russians drained more from Germany than the British and Americans were putting in, to saddling the West with the burden of relief for people who lived in an impoverished economy.

To establish a fair priority system for demobilization, the Army devised the discharge-point method. To get his "ruptured duck" discharge button (below), a soldier had to have a certain number of points. The biggest point getters were dependent children. The happy father in the cartoon is saying, "Come to Daddy, ya wonderful little twelve-point rascal."

On May 3, 1946, less than a year after V-E Day, General Lucius Clay, the deputy American commander in Germany, suspended delivery of reparations to the Russians until the Soviets agreed to operate their zone as part of a united Germany. The U.S.S.R. had not only converted its zone into a Communist satellite but had rejected Byrnes's unprecedented offer of a 25-year alliance against German militarism. As the Americans and British despaired of reaching an agreement with the Russians, they eased their occupation policies and took steps to make the German economy self-sustaining.

Clay's decision indicated a new hardening of American policy toward the U.S.S.R. The United States was irritated not only by Soviet intransigence in Germany but by Russia's attempt to extend its influence into the Middle East by exerting pressure on Iran and Turkey. By January 1946 Truman was writing, "Unless Russia is faced with an iron fist and strong language another war is in the making. . . . I'm tired of babying the Soviets."

Truman's determination to pursue a "get tough" policy with the Russians led him in March 1946 to accompany Winston Churchill to Fulton, Missouri, where the former prime minister delivered a major address in the gymnasium of Westminster College. The British leader declared: "From Stettin in the Baltic to Trieste in the Adriatic, an iron curtain has descended across the

Continent. Behind that line lie all the capitals of the ancient states of central and eastern Europe." To curb the Kremlin's "expansive tendencies," Churchill urged an Anglo-American "fraternal association." There was nothing the Russians admired, he said, "so much as strength, and there is nothing for which they have less respect than for . . . military weakness."

America was not ready for such blunt talk. The Boston *Globe* rejected Churchill's invitation "to become heir to the evils of a collapsing colonialism." The Chicago *Sun* said: "To follow the standard raised by this great but blinded aristocrat would be to march to the world's most ghastly war."

It was the knowledge that the A-bomb might result in "the world's most ghastly war" that made some Americans hesitate to accept the fact that the world was divided into two political spheres or to approve appropriate military preparations. Instead, the country urged the President to continue to pursue ways to end the threat of the bomb. On June 14, 1946, the American delegate Bernard Baruch proposed to the first session of the United Nations Atomic Energy Commission the creation of an international atomic development authority, to which America would turn over its atomic secrets—provided that there be effective international control and inspection of bomb production. Under this plan, there would be no further manufacture of bombs, and existing stocks would be destroyed. "We are here," Baruch declared, "to make a choice between the quick and the dead." The Soviet Union quickly erased all hope for effective control by insisting that the United States demolish stockpiles *before* a system of inspection was set up, and by stipulating that the veto be retained in the international atomic agency.

Before Herbert Lehman became head of UNRRA, he served for 10 years as governor of New York. Concern over state finances led Lehman to call his new dog Budget. Later, Budget's puppies were dubbed Surplus and Deficit by newsmen eager to see which grew bigger. Surplus won—and Lehman changed a $107 million budget deficit to an $80 million surplus.

THE attempt to halt the atomic arms race had failed. The United States had already set up an atomic program, and in the absence of an international agreement, it pushed forward on its own with the secret development of nuclear energy under an Atomic Energy Commission. The McMahon Act established the principle that the government should have an absolute monopoly of fissionable materials, and that the program should be run by civilians.

In the summer of 1946 the United States conducted atomic tests at the Bikini atoll in the Pacific. The results were awesome. Dr. David Bradley, who was involved in the tests, wrote a book, *No Place to Hide*, which told what the scientists found after Bikini—the sides of ships so charged with radioactivity that only sandblasting would clean it away, rocks miles from the blast charged with deadly particles. "The question," Dr. Bradley wrote, "is not political so much as biological. It is not the security of a political system but the survival of the race that is at stake."

Many Americans were deeply troubled by the point to which the world had come in the summer of 1946. It was hard to remember now the happy expectations of only 12 months before. Most of the trouble had been precipitated by the Russians, but not a few Americans were worried by the bleak consequences which might follow from the Truman-Byrnes "get tough" approach. To many, America's new foreign policy—A-bombs, verbal threats, the contemplated *rapprochement* with the former enemy Germany against the wartime ally Russia—seemed destined to plunge the United States into a fearful war with the Soviet Union.

No one was more troubled than Secretary of Commerce Henry Wallace, who, as former Vice President under Franklin Roosevelt, personified the

In the grotesque parade of criminals at the Nuremberg Trials was Hermann Goering. He testified with arrogant candor, announcing his own conception of totalitarianism: "The opposition of each individual person was not tolerated unless it was a matter of unimportance." Goering's final defiance was to cheat the hangman at the last minute by poisoning himself.

liberal tradition of the Roosevelt years. On July 23, 1946, Wallace wrote Truman that he was disturbed by the size of military appropriations; an arms race, he warned, would eventually lead to a situation where several nations had the bomb and the world would be prey to "a neurotic, fear-ridden, itching-trigger psychology." Instead of an extensive arms program, Wallace wished to develop trust in the U.S.S.R. by recognizing its power and allaying what he felt were its many reasonable suspicions.

Wallace's letter made small impression. On September 6, 1946, Byrnes made a speech in Stuttgart which indicated America's determination to rebuild Western Germany. Six days later Wallace addressed a Democratic rally at New York's Madison Square Garden. His speech was a blunt attack on Byrnes's policy. "We have no more business in the political affairs of Eastern Europe than Russia has in the political affairs of Latin America, Western Europe and the United States," Wallace said. Although the speech was not wholly one-sided, Wallace not only omitted two references in the prepared draft that were critical of the Communists, but interpolated: "I realize that the danger of war is much less from Communism than it is from imperialism." He said that he was "neither anti-British nor pro-British, neither anti-Russian nor pro-Russian," and added pointedly: "When President Truman read these words, he said that they represented the policy of his Administration."

Truman had, in fact, told reporters that he approved Wallace's speech, but in the ensuing uproar the President apparently had second thoughts. Secretary Byrnes, still in Europe, was incensed. He wired the President: "If it is not completely clear in your own mind that Mr. Wallace should be asked to refrain from criticizing the foreign policy of the United States while he is a member of your Cabinet, I must ask you to accept my resignation immediately." A little before 10 o'clock on the morning of September 20, Truman phoned Wallace: "Henry, I am sorry, but I have reached the conclusion that it will be best that I ask for your resignation." Truman proceeded to make an unhappy situation even worse by asking the country to accept the unlikely story that he had never approved the speech in the first place.

TRUMAN had supported Byrnes in his dispute with Wallace, but the President was far from happy with his Secretary of State. He resented Byrnes's cavalier manner of reporting to the White House; his subordinate appeared to feel that he had more right to be in the presidential office than Truman had. When, in January of 1947, Byrnes resigned because of ill health, Truman was delighted to name General George Catlett Marshall in his place.

On February 24, 1947, barely a month after he took office, Marshall was confronted with the greatest crisis in foreign affairs since the end of the war. On that day the British ambassador revealed that within six weeks financial troubles would compel Britain to cut off its aid to Greece and Turkey. Rarely in human events has there been so dramatic an occasion as this decision by one power to turn over the reins to another. From the Indian Ocean to the Mediterranean, British authority was dissolving. If the United States did not assume the burden, dire results could be foreseen. Greece would fall to the Communist bands that were sustained by Russian satellites on its borders; Turkish resistance would falter; Iran would be encircled; and no one knew if Europe could sustain the shock of seeing the Soviets break through to the Mediterranean and the Persian Gulf.

Truman, supported by Marshall and his aides, instantly recognized the nature of the crisis. But he faced formidable obstacles in persuading a country already suspicious of the "get tough" policy that the United States should take on the unpopular job of carrying on Britain's imperial policies in Greece. Senator Vandenberg, aware of the problem, advised: "Mr. President, if that's what you want, there's only one way to get it. That is to make a personal appearance before Congress and scare hell out of the country."

ON March 12, 1947, the President went before Congress to ask for $400 million for economic and military aid to Greece and Turkey. In presenting what quickly became known as the "Truman Doctrine," the President declared: "I believe that it must be the policy of the United States to support free peoples who are resisting attempted subjugation by armed minorities or by outside pressures."

Truman's tough address stirred up a storm of debate. Liberals, critical of Greek and Turkish leaders, objected that the Truman Doctrine proposed to fight totalitarianism by associating the United States with the defense of totalitarian regimes. Yet in the end most such critics swung to the support of the Truman Doctrine, however reluctantly. Although conservatives claimed that liberals were "soft on Communism," a majority of liberals in Congress voted in favor of foreign-policy measures to check the Russians.

Ironically, many of the most vigorous objections to the Truman Doctrine and similar proposals came from the other end of the political spectrum. Though many conservatives in Congress were vocally anti-Communist, they were unwilling to appropriate funds to contain the Soviets. They feared that unbalanced budgets would bankrupt the nation and lead to a Communist triumph. To avoid the expensive commitment required by the Truman Doctrine, Republican critics—not previously considered ardent admirers of the U.N.—argued that the President was "bypassing the U.N." But the adroit Senator Vandenberg marshaled enough Republican votes to win approval for the Greek-Turkish aid bill.

In its initial test, the Truman Doctrine proved singularly successful. An American mission, financed by Truman Doctrine funds, helped bolster the Greek economy and reorganize the army. Both nations ultimately were saved from Communist domination. Yet the critics of the Truman Doctrine objected that it was essentially a negative response which left the initiative in foreign affairs to the Russians and which encouraged a warlike posture toward the Soviet Union. In a speech in Columbia, South Carolina, Bernard Baruch used a new phrase to describe the deterioration of Soviet-U.S. relations: "Let us not be deceived—today we are in the midst of a cold war."

The Truman Doctrine had been an emergency response to an emergency situation in the "Cold War." Marshall had already taken steps to develop a more fruitful long-range policy. After he took over the State Department, a Policy Planning Staff was set up, and the world-wise George Kennan, a 20-year veteran of the diplomatic corps who was one of the State Department's few Russian experts, was named to head it.

Kennan took a hardheaded look at the nature of Soviet-American relations. In an article published soon afterward he said that United States policy should be one of "long-term, patient but firm and vigilant containment of Russian expansive tendencies"—by force if necessary, but always leaving the

"Don't mind me—just go right on talking."   FEB. '47

Long before Russia detonated a nuclear device, cartoonist Herbert Block felt it was impossible for the U.S. to maintain a permanent monopoly in atomic weapons, and here he warned of the worldwide menace of the bomb. The patently nonalignable Mr. Atom, cast as an undertaker, measures the earth for a coffin while he addresses a stubborn group of negotiators.

way open for the U.S.S.R. to submit without losing too much face. By Kennan's reckoning, a successful policy of containment would force the Kremlin to adopt a more circumspect policy and "promote tendencies which must eventually find their outlet in either the breakup or the gradual mellowing of Soviet power." With some modification, Kennan's views guided American policy toward Russia well into the 1960s.

Marshall also directed the Policy Planning Staff to study what could be done to save Western Europe from ruin; the only condition he laid down was "Avoid trivia." Some drastic solution was desperately needed. By 1947 Europe was on the verge of breakdown. The end of lend-lease had created an international economic crisis. Allied nations owed the United States $11.5 billion for goods they had acquired but could not pay for. To close this "dollar gap," the United States resorted to emergency measures—such as a $3.75 billion loan to Britain in 1946—but these brought only momentary relief. Although the United States by the middle of 1947 had given $10 billion to Europe, the European economy was collapsing and the people faced starvation. In March 1947 the situation became perilous when UNRRA drew toward its end at the very time that Europe was reeling from the blows of a vicious winter.

It was to this new crisis that Kennan and the Policy Planning Staff turned their attention. In May 1947 they sent Marshall their recommendation: an offer of massive American economic aid to Europe on condition that the Europeans take the initiative in working out the details of the program. The policy planners favored a program that was not set within a framework of anti-Communism, but of America's willingness to take the lead in stamping out hunger and poverty. They believed that military measures alone would not contain Communism, that it was crucial to deal with the economic dislocations and the "profound exhaustion of physical plant and of spiritual vigor," which the Communists could exploit.

Sarcastically captioned "Helpful Uncle Sam," these cartoons from the semiofficial Soviet magazine "Krokodil" accompanied an editorial which damned the Marshall Plan as cynical and selfish. In typical party-line distortions, Uncle Sam remarks above, "Why bother strengthening your currency—use mine," while below he says, "Don't sow wheat—I'll sell you corn."

IN a historic speech at Harvard University on June 5, Secretary Marshall spelled out the program. He offered economic aid to all nations which would co-operate, not excluding the Soviet Union. "Our policy," the Secretary declared, "is directed not against any country or doctrine, but against hunger, poverty, desperation and chaos." The plan proposed that the nations, instead of approaching the United States with separate shopping lists, should decide among themselves how resources were to be allocated. By placing the responsibility on Europe, the United States was ridding itself of the onus of bickering or delays and of the charge of American domination.

No one anticipated the swift European response to the Marshall Plan. In London Foreign Secretary Ernest Bevin stated: "This is the turning point." Within 22 days the British, French and Russians were meeting in Paris. But in the midst of discussions Molotov received word from Moscow that he was to pull out. Thereafter the Kremlin denounced the Marshall Plan as a capitalist plot; once again a wedge had been driven between East and West. The other European nations, 16 in all, presented the United States with a four-year plan of economic rehabilitation which would cost $22 billion (the Administration pared this estimate to $17 billion). At the end of four years these countries were to be economically self-supporting.

It was a breathtaking program, and many anticipated that Europe's hopes would be dashed by opposition in America to spending such an astronomic sum. Henry Wallace, more and more echoing the line of Communist advisers, denounced the proposal as a "Martial Plan," while Robert Taft spoke for Republican conservatives who complained that the plan would bankrupt the United States and that it ignored Asia.

Taft's opposition provided an acid test for Vandenberg's ability to hold the Republicans to a bipartisan foreign policy. (At one point ex-isolationist Vandenberg wrote to his wife regarding Republican opposition to the plan: "I get so damned sick of that little band of G.O.P. isolationists who are always in the way that I could scream.") But he made the kinds of concessions to the isolationists which conceded nothing in substance but which won the necessary votes. Even with Vandenberg's skill at compromise, the issue was long in doubt. The Russians inadvertently came to the plan's aid. On February 25, 1948, Communists seized control of the Republic of Czechoslovakia, which had been regarded as a bridgehead between East and West, and Jan Masaryk, son of the founder of the republic, died under mysterious circumstances. A new Soviet threat toward Finland, and fear that Italy would go Communist in its upcoming elections, also served to win support for the Marshall Plan. Yet the argument in support of the plan also altered; it came to be portrayed simply as an anti-Soviet stratagem. To beat the deadline of the Italian elections, the Senate met in night sessions. It finally passed the bill by the impressive majority of 69-17. The House quickly gave its approval, and on April 3, 1948, the Marshall Plan became law.

George F. Kennan proved his insight into Soviet affairs years before he outlined the policy of "containing" Communism. Well versed in Russia's language, history and psychology, he had warned against Stalin's duplicities as early as 1933. Accounting for his preoccupation with Russia, Kennan said he "must have lived before and been a Russian."

THE plan was a stunning success. It met and surpassed every production target. Its funds were put to work to build dikes in the Netherlands, drain malarial swamps in Sardinia, build railroads in Turkey and erect steel mills in France. By 1950 the dollar gap was down to a postwar low of two billion dollars. By 1952 production in Europe was 200 per cent higher than in 1938. Even though most of the benefits of the plan were siphoned off by the wealthier classes in such countries as France and Italy, an economic base was built upon which future reforms could be grounded. The plan cost almost five billion dollars less than had been anticipated. Opponents had claimed that foreign aid would bankrupt the country, but during this period the United States enjoyed unparalleled prosperity—while winning incalculable good will abroad. The London *Economist* said: "Marshall aid is the most straightforwardly generous thing that any country has ever done for others."

For a brief season it seemed that Marshall aid would show the world the way toward peace, but as the Cold War intensified, America's foreign-aid goals took on a new military focus. In 1948 Congress had stipulated that not one penny of Marshall Plan funds was to be used for military purposes. But in 1951 America informed Europe that every penny would be allotted to aid Western defenses. By 1952 about 80 per cent of United States aid was going for military weapons, the other 20 per cent for defense support.

The new military objectives of the Marshall Plan were a response to Soviet aggressiveness in Europe and the Far East. The Marshall Plan had frustrated Soviet hopes that Western Europe would disintegrate. Even more troublesome to Russia was the renascence of Germany under the aegis of Western capitalist powers. The American and British zones had been forged into a single region of rich industrial resources, and in June 1948 the Allies carried out a drastic currency reform. These moves helped set off a remarkable

George C. Marshall, victorious general and Secretary of State, had the rare distinction of having graduated from the Virginia Military Institute without a demerit. To say that he never broke a rule would be incorrect: He risked being "busted" on many a moonless night when he slipped out of his barracks for rendezvous with a certain Lily Coles—his future wife.

According to a friend, soft-spoken General Lucius DuBignon Clay's great weakness was a tendency to forget that his mind worked four or five times faster than others'. Another general decided to see whether Clay's mental prowess equaled its reputation. He raced through a bulky report in half an hour and then handed it to Clay. Clay calmly read it in five minutes.

economic revival in Western Germany. At the same time, the Western powers encouraged the creation of a new, independent nation there. The Russians reacted by precipitating a quarrel that brought a real risk of war. The focus of the dispute was the old German capital of Berlin, which since 1945 had been occupied by all four powers as an enclave 110 miles behind the Iron Curtain. On June 24, after weeks of harassment of Western traffic into Berlin, the Soviets clamped a rail blockade on the Western sectors.

The Berlin blockade posed a thorny problem for Western leaders. Some wanted to ram an armored train through the Russian blockade. Others wanted to withdraw altogether to avoid the danger of war. But General Clay cabled: "IF WE MEAN . . . TO HOLD EUROPE AGAINST COMMUNISM, WE MUST NOT BUDGE . . . I BELIEVE THE FUTURE OF DEMOCRACY REQUIRES US TO STAY."

At the end of the first week of the blockade, Berlin had enough bread to last only 25 days; enough meat for 33 days. The air lanes seemed the only practical route to the city. Clay called General Curtis LeMay at U.S. Air Force headquarters in Wiesbaden: "Curt, can you transport coal by air?" After a startled pause, LeMay replied: "Excuse me, General, would you mind repeating that question?" Then LeMay rounded up all the planes in his command, including some old B-17 bombers. C-54 Skymasters were flown in from all over the world. By October 1948 the Berlin Airlift was carrying almost 5,000 tons into the city daily. Even those who had faith in the project were amazed by what they were accomplishing.

"But," wrote the *New Statesman and Nation* in London, "every expert knows that aircraft, despite their immense psychological effect, cannot be relied upon to provision Berlin in the winter months." Yet the remarkable ferry of planes continued through the Berlin winter. For months, Berliners lived with the incessant roar of the planes in their ears. So heavy was the traffic —one plane every three minutes—that a plane which could not land on the first attempt had to return all the way to its parent base.

B Y the spring of 1949, the achievements of the airlift erased any doubt that it would succeed. On one day, April 16, American and British flyers hit a record total of 12,941 tons, and it was clear they could keep it up forever.

On May 12, 1949, after 321 days, the Russians capitulated. Rail lines and highways to Berlin were reopened. At a meeting of the City Assembly, Mayor Ernst Reuter paid moving tribute to the 48 airmen who had been killed. The Assembly renamed the plaza in front of Tempelhof Airport "Platz der Luftbrücke" (Airlift Square) in commemoration.

The Soviet Union had sustained an unmitigated defeat. Instead of driving the West out of Europe, it had welded the United States and the Western European nations more closely together. And something even more significant had happened. The tactics of the Kremlin had dissolved the spirit of the old wartime alliance against Germany once and for all. Correspondent Theodore H. White noted a "curious change in phraseology" during the airlift. "When, at a bar in the Ruhr or Frankfurt, one heard Americans use the pronoun 'they,' 'they' almost invariably referred to the Germans, still the enemy to be watched and controlled. But at a bar or over dinner in Berlin when one heard 'they,' 'they' almost invariably referred to the Russians. The Germans were included in 'we.'"

By now events in Europe had convinced leaders of the need to organize some kind of regional alliance to prepare against possible Russian aggression. In March 1948 Britain, France, Belgium, the Netherlands and Luxembourg had signed the Brussels Pact, pledging military aid to any member under attack. A year later, while the Berlin blockade was still in effect, the United States signed the North Atlantic Treaty with the five Brussels Pact nations, plus Canada, Italy, Norway, Portugal, Denmark and Iceland. (In 1952, Greece and Turkey joined; in 1955, West Germany.) Article 5 of the NATO treaty stipulated that "an armed attack against one or more of the signatories in Europe or North America shall be considered an attack against them all."

Not since the Convention of 1800, when the United States freed itself from the alliance with France, had the American government agreed in peacetime to a treaty of alliance outside the Western Hemisphere. Nothing indicated so clearly the end of isolationism in the United States.

Almost all of the foreign policy of the postwar years had been directed at stabilizing Western Europe. Now, with Western Europe reasonably secure, Washington could turn its attention to the uncommitted regions of Asia and Africa as well as Latin America. When President Truman delivered his inaugural address in 1949, the fourth point of his international recommendations was "a bold new program" to help the underdeveloped areas of the world free themselves of poverty and exploitation. The United States government would provide technical assistance and encourage investment abroad.

By 1952 America's "technical missionaries" were working in 33 nations. A former county agent from Tennessee helped increase wheat output in the Ganges plain; a Georgian bounced over the Iranian roads in a jeep, spreading the gospel of literacy; a team from Oklahoma A & M set up an agricultural secondary school in Ethiopia.

Despite these achievements, Point Four was longer on promise than on fulfillment. Private investment proved disappointingly small. Congress showed little interest in a costly foreign-aid program which might go on for years and which had no predictable relation to national security. Like Marshall aid, Point Four, too, was quickly transformed into a weapon of the Cold War.

Five years after the *Queen Mary* steamed into New York harbor with its burden of returning soldiers, the postwar world had taken a shape quite unanticipated on that sunny afternoon in 1945. The wartime alliance with Soviet Russia had been shattered and the two great powers were engaged in a Cold War that might, at any moment, erupt into a hot one. America's frontiers were now on the Elbe and the Bosporus. Leaders of both American parties had become committed to Kennan's doctrine of "containment"—of meeting Russian expansion with force or the threat of force.

The Cold War had divided the world into two armed camps. Every American move in foreign policy was now weighed for its military consequences. Yet despite this heavy reliance on military power, the United States was in a vulnerable position—particularly if the Soviet Union decided to start a war in a marginal area in which the United States would not wish to use an atomic bomb, a war which the United States would be ill equipped to fight. Such a war, particularly if it could not be fought through to final and decisive victory, might unleash all the angry, explosive feelings which the country harbored about the overwhelming experience of the postwar years—the years when the nation's bland confidence in its military security vanished forever.

The round-the-clock roar of the 11-month airlift gave to the people of Berlin a profound awareness that they "were not alone." When severe weather conditions or a mishap caused a momentary lull in air traffic, there was "a paralyzing silence . . . the silence of a corpse." When the roar could be heard again, "a hundred thousand sighs of relief" rose from the city.

An epochal revolution in science

THE paradox of the nuclear age is that it began in 1945 with a vision of the Inferno and was transformed with astonishing speed into the most creative scientific era the world has ever known. Indeed, technology advanced further in the two decades following Hiroshima than in any comparable period in man's history. Scientists synthesized wonder drugs that ended the threat of terrible diseases, created transistors that opened new vistas in electronics, produced exotic fuels to propel even more exotic space vehicles. Giant computers unraveled in minutes millions of complex mathematical problems that would take men hundreds of years to solve. Using atomic tracers, researchers studied the submicroscopic world seeking the explanation of dreaded illnesses like cancer. Radioisotopes (beneficial by-products of bomb making) soon found life-giving use in destroying malignant growths. A fresh vocabulary sprang up to describe the new discoveries. Almost everyone had some idea of what was meant by terms like automation, miniaturization and laser. Adults discussed the difference between fusion and fission; children, watching television, clocked the countdowns in the U.S. space-flight program.

The scientists, long portrayed as absent-minded and impractical tinkerers, emerged as heroes of the postwar United States. The demigods of sport and the matinee idols of the movies had to make way for intense, reserved men like Dr. Jonas Salk *(below)*, developer of the famous polio vaccine. The ordered life of the laboratory was disrupted by the homage of a grateful nation.

PROTECTION against polio is conferred on a child by Dr. Jonas Salk, discoverer of the Salk vaccine. During trials of the vaccine in 1954, thousands of elementary-school pupils were innoculated. The vaccine proved highly effective against paralytic polio, the type most feared during epidemics. By 1960, it had helped reduce cases to some 2,200 from 18,000 in 1954.

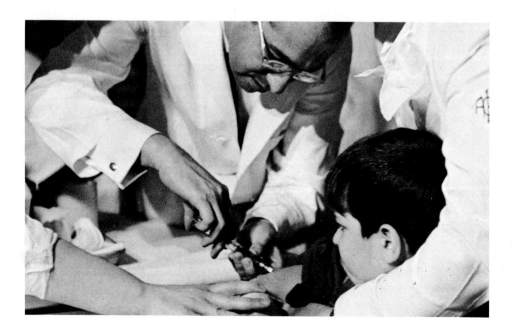

AWESOME DESTRUCTION by the hydrogen bomb is demonstrated during its first test on November 1, 1952, when it destroyed an entire island in the Pacific. Within a decade, even this weapon was dwarfed by H-bombs 15 times its size. But with the signing of a test-ban treaty in 1963, it seemed less likely that man would explode these ultimate weapons in anger.

A patch of daylight circling his eye, Commander James Calvert peers through the periscope of the atomic submarine U.S.S. "Skate." The vessel,

commissioned in 1957, can go 60,000 miles without refueling.

Atomic energy for engines of peace and defense

ALMOST as soon as the first atomic bomb was exploded in 1945, the U.S. began to harness the immense power of the atom. By the early 1960s nuclear-powered spacecraft of 380 tons were in the planning stage; nuclear-powered surface vessels were plying the seas and an impressive atom-powered submarine force was in being. Nine years after the pioneer *Nautilus* entered service in 1954, the Navy had in commission 30 nuclear submarines (13 of them armed with long-range Polaris missiles) capable of cruising submerged for months.

By 1963 cheap electricity from atomic energy was no longer a distant dream. Eleven nuclear power plants were in operation and another eight under construction. The largest of those blueprinted would generate more than a million kilowatts of power. They also generated controversy: Nervous neighbors often protested the proximity of radioactive products—despite the near-perfect safety record of U.S. atomic installations.

A NUCLEAR POWER PLANT near Rowe, Massachusetts, can produce 185,000 kilowatts of power for one year before refueling—and almost as cheaply as New England's conventional plants.

A PLEXIGLAS BUBBLE tops a tower at Wilkes Station, a U.S. base in the Antarctic. The dome protected scientists from the cold and wind as they studied phenomena like the aurora.

Probing the edges of space and the oceans' depths

IN 1957 the International Geophysical Year (IGY), to which the U.S. contributed some $500 million and 10,000 men, was launched as a gigantic collective assault on the secrets of the land, sea and air. For 18 months IGY scientists from 66 nations, based at 4,000 major outposts around the globe, sent out 70 ships and hundreds of balloons, rockets and satellites to gather information. In the atmosphere, IGY's fact-finding vehicles took the first photographs of the earth's cloud cover, learned how hurricanes are formed, charted wind circulation 40 miles above the earth. Satellites measured the intensity and distribution of the sun's energy and the amount of radiation the earth bounces back into space. Oceanographers made startling new discoveries, such as the existence of a 200-mile-wide current, deep beneath the surface of the Pacific, that travels eastward some 7,000 miles and carries a thousand times as much water as the Mississippi. In the Antarctic, where temperatures may drop to –125°F. and winds whip across the ice at 200 mph, the U.S. established a chain of communities from which teams of technicians emerged to collect data on everything from penguin migrations and the earth's magnetic field to earthquakes and weather patterns.

A BULBOUS NOSE on the bow of the Woods Hole Oceanographic Institute's 200-foot vessel, *Atlantis II*, allows scientists to observe undersea life through its glass portholes.

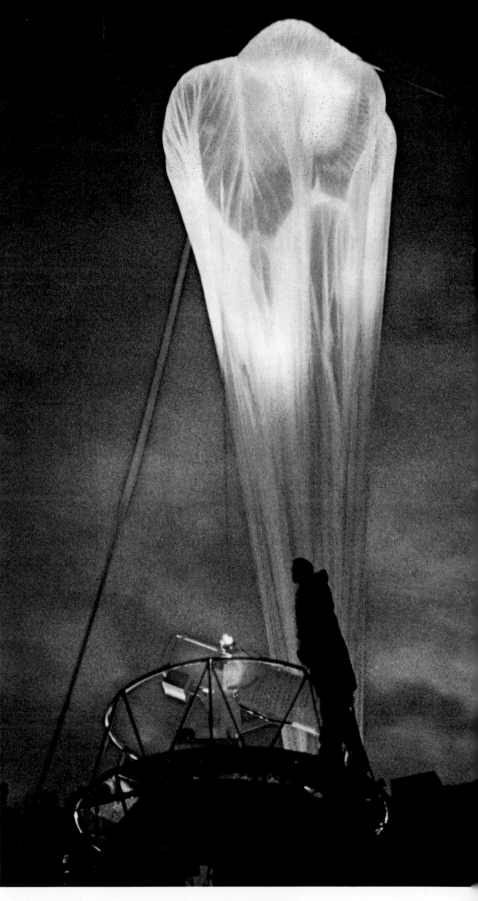

A HUGE BALLOON, some 170 feet in diameter when inflated, is shown at a Navy launching site in South Dakota. Its flight in 1959 produced valuable data on the planet Venus' atmosphere.

25

A SPECK no bigger than the D on a dime replaces four transistors and two resistors in a complex "flip-flop" circuit used in a Fairchild computer. It cost less, worked better, than the parts it replaced.

Tiny parts for complex tasks;
a new kind of light

ONE of the most startling technological developments of the '50s was in microelectronics. By reducing bulky vacuum tubes to clusters of pea-sized transistors, scientists introduced a cheaper, lighter, faster, more accurate system for controlling machines as varied as hi-fi sets, missiles, airplanes and computers.

No less striking is the laser (an acronym for "light amplification by stimulated emission of radiation"). Unlike natural light, a laser beam *(below)* does not diffuse its rays in all directions, but retains its tremendous power even when projected over long distances. Feasible applications for the laser include surgery, accurate cutting of the hardest metals and improved communications, with a single beam carrying more radio messages than all conventional radio channels combined.

A BEAM of ruby-red laser light bores a pin-point hole through a steel razor blade in a thousandth of a second. In operation the beam heats the steel to a temperature of some 10,000°F.

Telstar, Tiros, Mariner and Echo: new names in space

TRANSMISSION OF IMAGE of the Presidents carved on Mount Rushmore, South Dakota, forms part of the 1962 live television hookup, via *Telstar*, between the U.S. and 16 European nations.

ON July 10, 1962, *Telstar*, a gleaming satellite crammed with electronic gear, bounced a bright, clear image of Vice President Johnson from Washington, D.C., to Europe, thus completing the first live television broadcast across the Atlantic. Coming after a string of anticlimactic "seconds" in the space race, this feat proved that the U.S. had achieved world superiority in sophisticated space technology, although the Soviets still held the edge in big-thrust man carrying rocketry.

As the *Tiros* weather satellites and the *Echo* communication vehicle dependably transmitted information gathered during orbits around the earth, the spectacular *Mariner II* took a four-month, 180-million-mile journey toward Venus, relaying mountains of scientific data before radio contact was broken. To keep track of these and future generations of manned and unmanned satellites, the U.S. began constructing a network of weblike radio transmitter-receivers like the huge structure at left.

SEEKING SIGNALS, this giant radio transmitter and receiver *(left)* at Goldstone, California, scans the skies beneath a full moon. The concave surface helps locate and guide satellites.

TESTING COMPONENTS of satellites used in U.S. space probes, like *Ranger II* seen in the foreground, skilled technicians seek to avoid a repetition of failures that had occurred in the past.

Breakthroughs in healing

Inspired by the successes of penicillin during World War II, medical researchers studied some 3,500 antibiotics and by the mid-'50s had introduced 17 for routine cures of a battery of ills, from skin ulcers and rheumatic fever to mastoiditis and tuberculosis. Virologists developed vaccines against such bothersome

ailments as flu and measles. Tranquilizing drugs gave relief to many of the mentally ill, who were then able to leave institutions. In surgery, modern technology and human skill combined to achieve many near-miraculous innovations: successful transplants of corneas, arteries, bones and cartilages from one body to another; plastic sheaths to help severed arteries and nerves regenerate; dacron tubes to replace weak parts of the aorta. New, complex equipment allowed surgeons to perform open-heart operations while heart-lung machines, like the one in the foreground below, kept life in anesthetized patients.

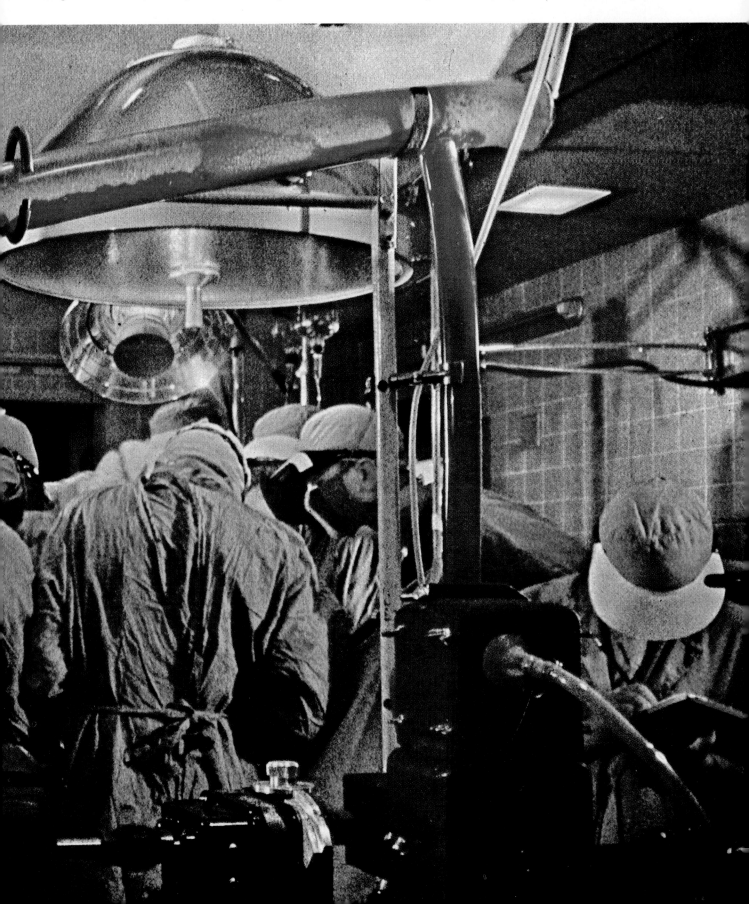

2. THE
FAIR DEAL

IN the era of free security that had existed before World War II, America had generally been able to seal off foreign affairs in a watertight compartment. In the Cold War this was no longer possible. Central to the containment theory was the belief that the United States must convince the world of its vitality as a free nation. Thus an economic recession could no longer be viewed merely as a matter of domestic concern, for it would cast doubt on America's ability to defend its allies. The attitude of the United States toward Negroes would be watched closely not only in American communities but in the capitals of the emerging Afro-Asian countries.

In the postwar years the United States rarely made a move in domestic affairs without looking into a mirror to see what kind of "image" it was presenting to the world. In the process the nation had to find the right answers to some hard questions. Could Americans master the new technology—involving everything from atomic energy to automation—or would they let it master them? Could they solve the vexing problem of relations between the races? Could they improve their standard of living and meanwhile extend the benefits of America's productivity to the rest of the world?

At the end of World War II, this last question troubled Americans most. Memories of the Great Depression were still fresh; many feared that when the United States "reconverted" to a peacetime economy, there would be a new army of up to 10 million unemployed. The first indications were not

MASONIC GRAND MASTER Harry Truman gazes from his favorite portrait, which only hints at the courage and determination that marked him as an effective President.

encouraging. Asked in 1943 about how to reconvert, aircraft manufacturer Donald Douglas responded: "You shut the damn shop up." Ten days after Japan accepted surrender terms, three million Americans had lost their jobs.

Well before the end of the war, Congress had turned its attention to easing the transition. It had, among other things, passed a "GI Bill of Rights"; between 1945 and 1952 the government spent $13.5 billion to school and retrain veterans under this measure. Other ex-servicemen were able to borrow money to set themselves up in business or farming.

Congressmen disagreed on the role government should play in relation to business. The Employment Act of 1946 charted a middle course. It did not specify that the federal government must be solely responsible for full employment, as some backers had urged, but it did establish a three-man Council of Economic Advisers to aid the President and issue an annual economic report. Congress thus left the main areas of economic decision to business but granted the government new responsibility for the health of the economy.

In a remarkably brief period this hybrid government-business operation brought the country through the dangers of reconversion and carried the economy to a new level of productivity. During the war, when Henry Wallace had called for a postwar economy of 60 million jobs, he was scoffed at for setting his sights so high. By July 1946, less than a year after V-J Day, 56.4 million Americans were at work; four years later the total was 62 million and national income had jumped to $242 billion from $181 billion in 1946.

The federal government underwrote the postwar expansion in a variety of ways: farm price supports; long-term, low-interest GI mortgages; minimum wages. Billions of dollars were extended in consumer credit, much of it based on government securities held by financial institutions. Government spending during the war for new plants provided a basis for the vast expansion. At the end of the war the government owned 50 per cent of the country's machine-tool capacity, 70 per cent of the aluminum capacity, 90 per cent of synthetic rubber and magnesium processing capacity. The corporations operating these plants were able to buy most of them on very favorable terms.

But the impressive postwar expansion cannot be explained solely by the intervention of the federal government. By 1948 private capital was being invested in an explosive fashion, at an average three times that of 1929. No less important was the pent-up demand for consumer goods at the end of the war: Americans had come out of the war with $44 billion in savings, and they were itching to spend it.

Indeed, inflation soon became more of a problem than the anticipated depression. A tremendous pressure developed to lift all controls—and quickly. The country was tired of going without gasoline, of carrying around ration books, of eating liver instead of steak. American businessmen, after nearly nine years of New Deal regulations, had had to accept four years more of wartime controls, and they wanted to get back to "normal."

TRUMAN faced an impossible task. He had to manage the transition from a war to a peace economy at the same time that the country was moving back toward a quasi-war economy because of developments abroad. Called on to get rid of controls and yet prevent inflation, he succeeded only in making a difficult situation worse. For weeks he permitted two of his subordinates to war over the issue without indicating what he wanted. Chester Bowles,

"You folks hear any talk about a housing shortage?"   AUG. '47

It took extreme optimism to ignore the nation's housing problem in 1947. Yet federal action was so slow that Herblock's cartoon of a congressional investigator had a point. The government's figures revealed there were nearly six million families living doubled up, two million farm homes unfit to live in and another seven million city dwellings ripe for demolition.

director of the Office of Price Administration, opposed large price boosts, while John Snyder, a Missouri banker the President named director of the Office of War Mobilization and Reconversion, claimed that price rises would stimulate production. When Truman did act, he came down on the side of Snyder.

Truman was already under fire from conservatives for advancing a domestic program squarely in the New Deal tradition. Now his support of Snyder over Bowles threatened to cost him liberal support as well. From the outset the New Deal Democrats had compared the new President's every move with Roosevelt's. In particular they questioned Truman's appointments. "The Truman inner circle is not vicious," noted an editor; "it is plodding, unimaginative, easily impressed by men who have 'met a payroll,' and deeply suspicious of 'intellectuals'—meaning creators of ideas." The Roosevelt people felt increasingly out of place in the Truman Administration, and many who had been with Roosevelt from the beginning—among them Frances Perkins and Henry Morgenthau Jr.—soon left the government.

When Truman named Edwin Pauley, a California oilman, to the post of Under Secretary of the Navy, Secretary of the Interior Harold Ickes rebelled. Ickes told a Senate committee that Pauley had pressed him to halt a suit claiming federal title to tidelands oil because it would hamper Democratic party fund raising—the "rawest proposition" he had ever heard, Ickes said. Truman suggested Ickes might be "mistaken"—whereupon the irascible Secretary of the Interior resigned.

Chester Bowles made a fortune as a partner in the advertising firm of Benton & Bowles. Before retiring at 40, he had coached comic Fred Allen and created a radio landmark, the "Maxwell House Showboat." Turning to public service, he soon became director of the OPA, where he fought rising prices from 1943 to 1946—the "battle of the century," he called it.

THE conflict between the President and the New Dealers came to a head in a quarrel over the nettlesome problem of the rights of union labor. After the war labor leaders demanded increased wages to make up for the drop in take-home pay caused by the loss of overtime hours. The Administration agreed, suggesting that the economy could stand a 24 per cent wage rise without a rise in prices. But business objected to keeping the lid on prices, and labor was not satisfied with 24 per cent.

On November 21, 1945, one of America's largest unions, the United Automobile Workers of the CIO, launched a 113-day strike against one of the country's wealthiest corporations, General Motors, and got a 17.5 per cent wage-and-fringe-benefit rise amounting to 19.5 cents an hour. The next February 800,000 steelworkers won an 18.5 cent boost in another strike. But industry in turn was permitted to jack up steel prices five dollars per ton.

Wages and prices now seemed likely to chase each other out of sight. A 59-day coal strike in the spring of 1946 ended only after Truman ordered government seizure of the mines. Mine leader John L. Lewis won most of what he demanded during government operation, but at the cost of mounting antiunion sentiment in the nation.

In the midst of the coal crisis came an even more serious development: the threat of the first total strike on the railroads since 1894. To head off the walkout, Truman took over the railroads. But on May 23, 1946, in defiance of the President, union leaders called a national rail strike, and 25,000 loaded freight cars were halted. With perishable food sidetracked, prices shot up, and there were runs on groceries. More than 90,000 passengers were marooned— war brides on their way west, baseball clubs traveling between cities, the Philadelphia Symphony on its way to San Francisco. In Europe hundreds of thousands faced starvation as shipments of food to Eastern ports were delayed.

Grimy with coal dust, John L. Lewis, president of the United Mine Workers of America, emerges from an Illinois mine. The 1946 strike he led enraged many but won a multimillion-dollar welfare fund for his union, raised by a royalty on every ton of mined coal. A lover of rhetoric, Lewis spoke sweepingly of labor as "18 million stomachs clashing against backbones."

Furious at rail union leaders, the President went before Congress on May 25 with a bombshell proposal: a request for authority to draft the workers into the armed forces. Halfway through his speech, Truman received a note announcing that the strike had been settled on his terms. But the President's proposal shocked Congress. It was denounced by senators running a spectrum from liberals like Claude Pepper ("I would give up my seat in the Senate before I would support this bill.") to conservatives like Robert Taft ("This proposal goes farther toward Hitlerism, Stalinism, totalitarianism than I have ever seen proposed in any strike.").

TRUMAN'S address appeared to have severed his last ties with liberals and labor. R. J. Thomas, national secretary of the CIO-PAC, took down the picture of the President and himself that hung on the wall over his desk and dropped it into a wastebasket. "Labor," he announced, "is through with Truman." Then, when Congress framed a milder labor bill, Truman antagonized conservatives by vetoing the measure as antilabor. Truman was now in trouble with all sides. Yet the President sensed correctly that if he did not curb wage rises, business demands for price concessions would seriously impair the effectiveness of the Office of Price Administration.

By the early summer of 1946, OPA was under heavy attack. Although rationing had been virtually abandoned and controls eased on over 4,000 items, foes of price control complained that OPA ceilings imposed hardships on farm and business interests. Price control was due for renewal July 1, 1946. Three days before the deadline Congress voted a new bill which ended many controls and provided for the rapid abandonment of others. Chester Bowles, now economic stabilization director, resigned in protest.

Truman vetoed the new bill—even though it meant that until Congress could be persuaded to pass a more satisfactory measure, there would be no price control at all. In the first 16 days of July, the prices of basic commodities jumped 25 per cent, about twice as much in two weeks as in the previous three years. Meat rose 20 cents a pound, corn 80 cents, rents 20 per cent in Chicago.

On July 25 Truman signed a new price-control bill, and in late August price ceilings were reimposed on selected items, including meat. Angry stockmen held back their cattle from market. The Armour meat company's main plant in Chicago, which normally handled 9,000 head of cattle a week, now received only 68. In New York City nine out of every 10 butcher shops closed down. By early October the country was swept by a frenzy of protest over the meat shortage. A New York *Times* headline read: "Queens Restaurateur, Worried Over Meat, Dives off Brooklyn Bridge." Charges were heard that American steaks were being sold on the European black market or had gone "into the larders of the Russians."

"The weird cry for 'meat,'" noted the astute newspaperman Tom Stokes, "seemed, as one heard it, to symbolize the desire for all things material." Although the shortage was the result of a strike of cattlemen, the country vented its anger not at them but at the government. Gallup polls showed that Truman's popularity had fallen from a peak of 87 to a lowly 32 per cent. The meat shortage coincided with the 1946 congressional and state election campaigns, and the Republicans made the most of it. Representative Charles Halleck, chairman of the Republican Congressional Campaign Committee, jeered that the Democratic election slogan should be "Let 'em Eat Horse

Meat." Alarmed Democratic leaders urged the President to lift controls.

On the night of October 14 Truman angrily announced in a radio address that since Congress had not given him adequate controls, and since the desire of cattlemen to "fatten their profits" had been fostered by conservatives, he now had no alternative but to end controls on meat. With decontrol, prices broke loose. When meat reappeared, steak cost one dollar a pound and up. Truman was now blamed for high meat prices.

The campaign of 1946 reflected widespread dissatisfaction in the nation. Labor resented Truman's handling of the rail strike; cattlemen and house-wives, his meat policy. Conservatives disliked his reform proposals, liberals doubted that these proposals were meaningful. On the advice of party leaders, Truman dropped out of the campaign, and the Democratic party played transcriptions of F.D.R.'s old campaign speeches over the radio instead.

When the ballots were counted that November it was clear that the country had gone to the polls in an ugly mood. Even Republicans were staggered by the dimensions of their victory. For the first time since 1930, they won control of both houses of Congress. Moreover, although some moderate Republicans won election, the majority of the new lawmakers were conservative, nationalistic men from the Midwest and the Far West. "Bring on your New Deal, Communistic and subversive groups," Ohio's new Senator John Bricker had announced during the campaign. "If we can't lick them in Ohio, America is lost anyway." In Wisconsin the 40-year-old La Follette dynasty in the Senate was terminated by a little-known 37-year-old veteran, Joseph McCarthy. (Among the notable newcomers to the House were two young men from opposite ends of the country: 29-year-old John F. Kennedy of Massachusetts, one of the few Democratic winners from the North, and 33-year-old Richard M. Nixon, a California Republican.)

ONE possible interpretation of the elections was that the Roosevelt coalition was falling apart. The Democratic party seemed to have lost its vitality. The bright young men who had built the New Deal alignment were now weary middle-aged men. The city machines which for so long had been the party's mainstay were old and flabby; the Republicans picked up five House seats in New York City, four each in Chicago and Los Angeles.

Most important, the elections appeared to be a brutal repudiation of President Truman's leadership. On the day after the election, Democratic Senator William Fulbright of Arkansas urged Truman to name a Republican Secretary of State as his successor and resign from office, and the usually responsible Chicago *Sun* and Atlanta *Constitution* called upon the President to adopt Fulbright's suggestion. Any possibility of Truman's re-election in 1948 now seemed out of the question.

To most observers that year the elections seemed to mark a turning point in the history of American politics, the point at which the Republican party had established its dominance for the next generation after 14 years out of power. A poll after the elections showed that only 8 per cent of the respondents thought the next President would be a Democrat.

The ideological significance of the 1946 elections seemed even more clear-cut: The country was in a conservative mood. But the same poll that predicted a Republican President in 1948 came up with some striking additional data. It found that Democratic voters who switched to the G.O.P. had no

During the mine strike of 1946, 3,000 coal cars stand empty at Williamson, West Virginia. Many cities and industries felt the effect. In Detroit, Ford shut up shop. Chicago turned off store and theater lights. Steel mills banked their fires. Many trains stopped running, and Washington was readying a freight-shipment embargo as the strike was settled.

desire to undo the New Deal reforms. All groups, including traditional Republicans, favored an extension of social security. Thus, there was ample evidence that if the Republicans actually interpreted the vote as a mandate for reaction, they would seriously imperil their fine chances for victory in 1948.

This is precisely what the Republicans of the 80th Congress did. They set about their tasks like a royalist faction returned from years of exile. Committee chairmen seized the opportunity to join with conservative Southern Democrats (numbering 100 of the 180 Democrats left in the House) to launch what was called a counter-revolution to the New Deal.

THE most imposing figure in the new Congress was the 57-year-old Republican senator from Ohio, Robert A. Taft. Taft appeared to be the epitome of conservatism. Testy, stiff in manner, he seemed to make a point of tactlessness, as though tact were an indication of dishonesty. He was respected even by his enemies for his earnestness and his industry, and he was probably the best-informed man in Congress. But he had a parochial image of both America and the world. Taft, someone observed, had the best mind in Washington, until he made it up.

Yet Taft was not the hidebound reactionary he was often thought to be. He sensed that the 1946 elections offered his party an opportunity to prove it could govern, and that the chance would be thrown away if the G.O.P. pursued the reactionary line advocated by such House leaders as Speaker Joseph W. Martin or by senators like his fellow Ohioan, Bricker. Taft sponsored modest proposals for federal aid to medical care, education and housing. "You don't get decent housing from the free-enterprise system," he explained with characteristic bluntness. By 1947 Bricker was complaining: "I hear the Socialists have gotten to Bob Taft."

On most issues it was the Brickers who dominated the 80th Congress. They rejected not only Truman's recommendations to extend social-security and minimum-wage legislation, but even Taft's moderate proposals. They slashed funds for power and reclamation projects in the West, for rural electrification, and for soil conservation and crop storage. They wreaked posthumous vengeance on Franklin Roosevelt in 1947 by adopting the 22nd Amendment, limiting all Presidents after Truman to two terms; ratification of the amendment was completed by the states in February 1951.

The response of the 80th Congress to the displaced-persons crisis was especially unfortunate. World War II and its aftermath had uprooted great multitudes of Europeans from their homes. Driven into exile, sometimes herded into Allied detention camps, many hundreds of thousands pleaded for admission to the United States. When in June 1948 Congress finally adopted a Displaced Persons Act to admit a scant 205,000 refugees, Truman signed the bill only "with very great reluctance"; the measure, he said, was "flagrantly discriminatory," for by stipulating that a high percentage of those admitted should come from the Baltic territories and should be farmers, the act effectively limited the immigration of Jews and Catholics.

In the 1946 campaign Republicans had claimed that the end of price control would end the nation's economic difficulties. Four days after the election, Truman surrendered to the opponents of controls. He took ceilings off everything but rents and two items in short supply: sugar and rice. As a result, prices rose between 1946 and 1947 more than they had in all of World

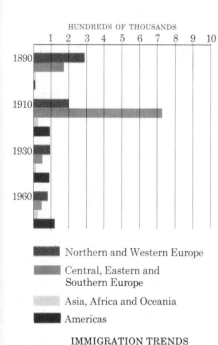

HUNDREDS OF THOUSANDS

IMMIGRATION TRENDS

IN KEY YEARS FROM 1890

Because of earlier restrictions, the largest single group of immigrants by the 1960s came from the Western Hemisphere. In 1890 most had been from northwestern Europe. In 1910 the great bulk was from the rest of Europe. In the 1920s, as the wave seemed due to resume soon after World War I, Congress passed tight quotas favoring northwestern Europeans—the group least anxious to come. One unexpected by-product was that industrial areas, cut off from unskilled European labor, hired more and more Negroes, thus speeding Negro migration from the South.

■ Northern and Western Europe

■ Central, Eastern and Southern Europe

■ Asia, Africa and Oceania

■ Americas

War II. In 1947 organized labor, its gains cut by inflation, demanded and won a second round of wage boosts, and in 1948 a third round. As the inflationary spiral mounted relentlessly, there were signs that people on fixed income and those in modest circumstances were losing faith in the Republican promise that laissez faire would solve the country's economic problems. A Gallup poll in August 1948 found that the country, by a surprisingly emphatic margin, favored the restoration of price controls and rationing.

Both Taft and the Bricker wing of the Republican party interpreted the 1946 election as a mandate to discipline labor unions. Much of the country, they believed, was exasperated with union abuses. After hearing out one labor delegation of 125 from his home state, Indiana's Senator William Jenner exploded: "You've come down here saying you want no legislation. . . . Well, by God, you're going to get some."

In April 1947 the House voted a tough labor bill, sponsored by Representative Fred A. Hartley Jr. of New Jersey. In the Senate liberal Democrats and Republicans forced Taft, chairman of the Labor Committee, to soften the measure. But the legislation approved in June was still stringent. The Taft-Hartley bill outlawed the closed shop (under which some employers had been required to hire only union members), curbed the union shop (under which new employees had to join the union) and encouraged states to adopt "right-to-work" laws which would forbid the union shop altogether. The measure forbade jurisdictional strikes and secondary boycotts, required union officials to file non-Communist affidavits, prohibited political contributions by unions to candidates for federal office, provided that unions register and report on their affairs, empowered the government to obtain injunctions against unions and stipulated a cooling-off period before walkouts.

Scottish-born Philip Murray, a coal miner at the age of 10 for 80 cents a day, became head of a United Mine Workers local and rose to be John L. Lewis' lieutenant in the UMW. Murray was later president of the United Steelworkers, then succeeded Lewis as head of the CIO after Lewis quit its presidency in a heated disagreement over national politics.

LABOR mounted a monumental campaign to persuade President Truman to veto the bill. National advertisements denounced it as a slave-labor measure. In New York City milk drivers left a veto appeal with each bottle of milk. The National Catholic Welfare Conference and Protestant and Jewish leaders urged a veto. At the White House mail trucks unloaded 800,000 letters.

On June 20, 1947, the President sent a 5,500-word veto message to Congress. After the first page, Hartley stopped listening; another Republican leader studiously read the Washington *Post's* comics. When the reading ended, there were cries of "Vote! Vote!" The House quickly overrode the veto. In the Senate liberals conducted the longest-sustained filibuster since 1927 in an attempt to prevent a vote; the body met in continuous session for almost 31 hours. When the filibuster broke down, the Senate voted to override by six votes more than needed.

The Taft-Hartley law was by no means the "slave-labor act" unions claimed it to be, but neither was it a balanced attempt at improving relations between labor and management. It imposed severe—and, in some respects, unworkable—restrictions on labor; from the political point of view it was a blunder, for it drove union labor, which had been antagonized by Truman in 1946, back into the arms of the Democratic party.

Of all the missed opportunities of the 80th Congress, none was so glaring as in the field of civil rights for Negroes. On this issue the Democrats, with their powerful Southern minority, were most vulnerable. But since the Republicans in the 80th Congress needed Southern Democratic support on conservative measures, and since many G.O.P. congressmen opposed federal intervention, no action was taken.

Where the Republicans feared to tread, President Truman, a descendant of Confederate sympathizers, stepped in. In December 1946 he set up a Presidential Committee on Civil Rights under the chairmanship of Charles E. Wilson, president of General Electric. After 10 months of study the committee issued a historic report. It recommended laws to protect individuals against police brutality, a federal antilynching statute, equal opportunity to vote, equal educational opportunity and federal action to end segregation. It advocated the creation of a permanent federal commission on civil rights and reorganization of the civil rights division of the Justice Department.

On February 2, 1948, President Truman sent a message to Congress which urged implementation of these recommendations. Southerners responded with a furious outburst of invective. Senator James Eastland of Mississippi declared: "The recommendations would destroy the last vestige of the South's social institutions and mongrelize her people."

At the White House in mid-March, Mrs. Lennard Thomas, Alabama Democratic National Committeewoman, told the President: "I want to take a message back to the South. Can I tell them you're not ramming miscegenation down our throats—and you're not for tearing up our social structure—that you're for all the people, not just the North?"

"Well, I've got the answer right here for you," the President said, and pulling a copy of the Constitution from his coat pocket, he proceeded to read her the Bill of Rights.

In the next few months Truman indicated that he favored modest advances in civil rights. But many of the Southern Democrats were adamant in their refusal to accept change. They launched a campaign to deny the presidential nomination to Truman; failing that, they made plans to bolt their party.

That summer the Democratic National Convention, after a stiff fight, voted to adopt a strong civil-rights plank. The stony-faced Mississippi delegation and 13 of the Alabama delegates marched out of the convention in protest, waving the Confederate flag. Five days later the bolters, widely known as Dixiecrats, met in Birmingham to form the States Rights party. Speakers warned that civil-rights legislation would result in the races "mingling in the beauty shops and the swimming pools." For presidential candidate, the convention named Governor J. Strom Thurmond of South Carolina; for Vice President, Governor Fielding Wright of Mississippi.

W HILE at one extreme the Dixiecrats were undercutting Truman's following in the South, at the other, critics of his foreign policy were threatening to deny him liberal support. When Truman forced him out of office, Henry Wallace announced: "I shall continue to fight for peace." Over the next year, as editor of the *New Republic*, Wallace assaulted Truman's foreign and domestic policies. On December 29, 1947, the former Vice President announced that he would run as an independent candidate for President. Seven months later Wallace's supporters founded the Progressive party. The Progressives denounced both major parties as warmongers and demanded the scrapping of the Truman Doctrine and the Marshall Plan. "The choice," announced the keynoter at the Progressive convention, "is Wallace or war."

Most liberal groups rejected the Wallace party, in part because Truman

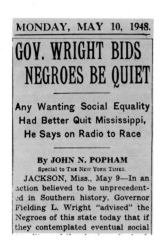

MONDAY, MAY 10, 1948.

GOV. WRIGHT BIDS NEGROES BE QUIET

Any Wanting Social Equality Had Better Quit Mississippi, He Says on Radio to Race

By JOHN N. POPHAM
Special to THE NEW YORK TIMES.

JACKSON, Miss., May 9—In an action believed to be unprecedented in Southern history, Governor Fielding L. Wright "advised" the Negroes of this state today that if they contemplated eventual social

The news story above and the Jim Crow sign below summed up the fanatical racist views of Mississippi Governor Fielding Wright, Dixiecrat candidate for Vice President in 1948. Wright opposed all attempts to end segregation, and said he was engaged in a fight for the "return to the States of powers illegally snatched from them . . . by a Washington bureaucracy."

THIS AREA IS & EXPECTS TO REMAIN A WHITE NEIGHBORHOOD
University Civic Club

showed a new commitment to liberal measures in 1948, but even more because they disapproved the pivotal role played by the Communists within the Progressive party. Under the guidance of men like Representative Vito Marcantonio of New York, the new party had adopted a program which consistently followed the Communist line. Wallace himself, while clearly no Communist, openly welcomed their support.

With the Democratic coalition disintegrating, the Republicans contemplated the 1948 campaign with even higher expectations than they had had after the rout of the Democrats in 1946. The center of Republican power lay in the rural, conservative hinterland, so it seemed that 1948 would be the year for Bob Taft to come into his own. But since 1936 the G.O.P., however conservative and isolationist its congressional delegation, had unfailingly turned to a man of moderately internationalist and liberal views for its presidential candidate. In 1948 it returned again to Thomas E. Dewey, who had been re-elected Governor of New York by a huge 680,000-vote margin in 1946. California's liberal Governor Earl Warren was picked as his running mate.

Jackie Robinson, the first Negro player formally admitted to major league baseball since the 1880s, signs a contract with the Brooklyn Dodgers, cued by Branch Rickey, then Dodger president. Although a few light-skinned Negroes played in the early 1900s billed as Cubans, Indians or Mexicans, the color line was not openly broken until Robinson was signed in 1945.

CERTAIN of victory, Dewey and his advisers treated the 1948 campaign as an ordeal that had to be undergone only because it was an American custom, not because it could affect the results. Dewey's cautious approach served to accentuate his colorlessness. Instead of making clear what he hoped to accomplish in office, he delivered speeches which abounded in platitudes: "Our future lies before us," or "We need a rudder to our ship of state. . . ." Dewey pursued the presidency, it was noted, with the "humorless calculation of a Certified Public Accountant in pursuit of the Holy Grail."

There was at least one man in the United States who believed Harry Truman could win, and that man was Harry Truman. On June 3, a month before the convention, Truman's train had departed Washington on a 9,500-mile "nonpolitical" swing around the country. Before leaving, the President told reporters: "If I felt any better I couldn't stand it." At first crowds were small, but after 10 days, people began to warm to him. Reporters noted a new campaign personality, "a blend of Will Rogers and a fighting cock." Truman was coming to find a winning appeal in assaults on the Republican 80th Congress. Stung by his rebukes, one G.O.P. congressman denounced the President as a "nasty little gamin." Truman was hitting with telling effect.

Most of the delegates in Philadelphia had not yet seen the "new Truman" in action. The President's acceptance speech electrified the convention. Truman aimed his main thrusts at the divergence between the promises in the G.O.P. platform and the performances of the Republican 80th Congress: "The Republican platform urges extending and increasing social security benefits. Think of that—and yet when they had the opportunity, they took 750,000 people off our social security rolls. I wonder if they think they can fool the people with such poppycock as that." Delighted with the new Truman, the crowd yelled, "Pour it on 'em, Harry!"

Truman had another surprise in store. In the same speech he announced to the startled but gleeful delegates that on July 26, the day turnips are planted in Missouri, he was going to summon the 80th Congress back into special session. "I'm going to call Congress back and I'm going to ask them to pass laws halting rising prices and to meet the housing crisis which they say they're for in their platform. At the same time I shall ask them to act on . . .

aid to education, which they say they're for; a national health program; civil rights legislation, which they say they're for . . . an increase in the minimum wage, which I doubt very much they're for . . . an adequate and decent law for displaced persons in place of the anti-Semitic, anti-Catholic law which this 80th Congress passed." He added: "They can do this job in 15 days if they want to do it." The convention was bedlam.

Not since 1856 had a President called back Congress in an election year. Critics denounced the President's move as blatantly political. "This petulant Ajax from the Ozarks," Republican Senator Styles Bridges of New Hampshire fumed, would find the "maddest Congress you ever saw." Bridges was right. "The Turnip Congress" passed nothing of consequence. But Truman had scored his point. He had switched the issue from Dewey's record to the hard-rock conservatism of the Republican Congress.

On September 17 when the President left Union Station, his running mate, Senator Alben Barkley of Kentucky, urged: "Mow 'em down, Harry." Truman responded: "I'm going to give them hell." In the next six weeks he traveled 22,000 miles and made 275 speeches. He jeered at Dewey's attempt to wage a campaign above issues ("He's been following me up and down this country making speeches about home and mother and unity and efficiency"). But he saved his most telling blows for the "do-nothing, good-for-nothing" 80th Congress and for the Republican party as the party of reaction.

In September both candidates were invited to address the National Plowing Contest at Dexter, Iowa. On the advice of his managers, Dewey declined. After all, Iowa had gone Democratic only three times since 1856, and polls showed him with 55 per cent of the vote in Iowa to Truman's 39 per cent. Truman accepted, and made the most of his opportunity. To a crowd of some 100,000 gathered at the Widow Agg's farm, the President declared that Congress had "stuck a pitchfork in the farmer's back."

Still almost no one thought Truman had a chance. Two months before Election Day, Elmo Roper stopped taking polls, noting that the heavy Dewey margin bore "an almost morbid resemblance to the Roosevelt-Landon figures as of about this time in 1936." Bookies quoted 1-15 odds that Dewey would win; in 1936, F.D.R. had been only a 1-3 favorite. Democratic leaders in Washington put their homes up for sale. The New York *Times* estimated that Dewey would receive 305 electoral votes, Truman 105, Thurmond 38, with 43 doubtful. There was one contrary note. When the Staley Milling Company of Kansas City offered its chicken feed for sale in bags marked with either a donkey or an elephant, 54 per cent chose the donkey sacks. The company thereupon discontinued its "pullet poll" because it did not believe its findings.

The Chicago "Tribune's" headline announcing Dewey's "victory" delighted a triumphant Harry Truman. In expectation of a G.O.P. landslide, a number of publications, including LIFE, *were published before the election with articles written as though Dewey had won. Pollster George Gallup, equally red-faced, announced a survey to determine "just what happened."*

ON election night people settled down before their radios anticipating an early bedtime, since Dewey's victory statement could be expected not long after the polls closed. At 9 p.m. Truman was ahead, but commentators explained that that was to be expected; the Democrats always took a lead in the cities—Truman would be snowed under when the rural areas began to report. At 10 p.m. farm regions were coming in; they were not so Republican as had been predicted, but still the cognoscenti were unperturbed. In Chicago newsboys hawked a *Tribune* extra with the headline: DEWEY DEFEATS TRUMAN.

At midnight the cities were continuing to pile up Truman majorities, and the countryside was still misbehaving, but the 70-year-old H. V. Kaltenborn, who ever since Munich had been the voice of authority on the airwaves, advised his listeners to keep waiting for those rural returns. Early in the morning announcers began to wonder: Would Dewey have enough votes for victory in the Electoral College or would the election be close enough to be thrown into the House? A while later their voices held a note of incredulity. Was it possible? Did Harry have a chance? At Republican headquarters at the Roosevelt Hotel in New York, Associated Press columnist Hal Boyle noted, the mood of the "victory" celebrants changed from confidence to surprise, "from surprise to doubt, from doubt to disbelief, and then on to stunned fear and panic." At 4:46 a.m. *Newsweek*, which was preparing an election extra on Dewey's victory, flashed a hold-everything order to its Dayton printing plant.

By dawn no one doubted that Truman had a chance; any of three large states would push him over. Some people, bleary-eyed and disbelieving, tried to catch a few winks. At breakfast they switched the radio on once more; Ohio was teetering back and forth. At 9:40 on a brilliant sunny morning, Democratic headquarters received a call from Columbus: Truman had only a paper-thin lead, but the districts still out were from Democratic Cuyahoga County. Ohio was safe. Yes, it was true; Truman had done it.

THOMAS E. DEWEY
REPUBLICAN

R EPUBLICANS were stunned, Democrats delirious. The country as a whole was immensely pleased with itself. In an age of conformity, it had bucked the tide and showed a defiant independence of the bandwagon psychology created by the national media. Taft might fume: "I don't care how the thing is explained. It defies all common sense for the country to send that roughneck ward politician back to the White House." A Buick dealer in Dewey's home town of Owosso, Michigan, might grumble: "There are just more damned fools in this country than there are intelligent people." But most Americans, quite apart from partisan beliefs, seemed to be delighted. The bumptious Mr. Truman had fooled them all: the smug retinue around Dewey, the wiseacre reporters, the intellectuals who thought they knew the country's heart and mind. The pollsters were crestfallen. George Gallup confessed: "I just don't know what happened. I have no alibi."

For the first time since 1916, a presidential candidate won with less than a majority of the popular votes. Truman received 24.1 million votes to his opponents' 24.2 million, but he scored a 303-189 advantage over Dewey in the Electoral College. The rebellion of the two extreme wings of the Democratic party may have helped Truman more than they hurt him. To be sure, Wallace's 1.2 million ballots (much fewer than anticipated, with no electoral votes) threw New York, Maryland and Michigan to the G.O.P., but the Wallaceite defection also made the Democrats less vulnerable to the charge that they were dominated by leftists. The States Rights movement cost the Democrats four Southern states (Thurmond, too, polled 1.2 million votes—and 39 electoral votes), but together with the strong civil-rights plank, it added to Truman's appeal to Negro voters and to friends of civil rights. One Negro editor commented on the Dixiecrat walkout: "Negroes felt if they didn't support Truman after that, no other politician would ever take such a stand." The Negro vote was crucial in several key states.

The big surprise of the election was the "green uprising" in the farm belt. Dewey carried only seven states between the Alleghenies and the Pacific. "Safely Republican" Iowa, which F.D.R. had lost to Dewey by 47,000 votes

HENRY A. WALLACE
PROGRESSIVE

J. STROM THURMOND
DIXIECRAT

Truman's chances for election appeared dim against the competition of this determined trio: Dewey, labeled a "limber trimmer" by H. L. Mencken; Wallace, who was leading a new "Gideon's army" to victory in the "century of the common man"; and Thurmond, who solemnly declared that the other three candidates hoped to give the country that "new Russian look."

in 1944, swung to Truman by a 28,000 margin. The Democrats won back both houses of Congress: the Senate by a margin of 12, the House by 92. Truman's assault on the 80th Congress had struck home. The Republican conservative bloc in the Senate was almost obliterated.

The Democratic party, which had appeared so moribund in 1946, suddenly came to life with the election of new men in the New Deal tradition. Illinois sent to the State House a 48-year-old newcomer to politics, Adlai Stevenson, and elected to the U.S. Senate Paul Douglas, a University of Chicago economics professor. The 37-year-old mayor of Minneapolis, Hubert Humphrey, was elected to the U.S. Senate in a campaign directed by 30-year-old Orville Freeman. The 37-year-old G. Mennen Williams, who one day would inherit a shaving-cream fortune, was elected governor of Michigan. Chester Bowles was chosen governor of Connecticut. Tennessee elevated Estes Kefauver from the House to the Senate; Texas did likewise for Lyndon Johnson.

On January 20, 1949, Harry Truman was inaugurated President in his own right. Washington celebrated the biggest, noisiest inauguration in history. Confident of a G.O.P. victory, the Republicans of the 80th Congress had appropriated a record $100,000 for the forthcoming inauguration; the Democrats were delighted to spend it. The presidential car drove down Pennsylvania Avenue flanked by an honor guard from Truman's World War I artillery unit, Battery D, and trailed by a calliope tooting, "I'm Just Wild About Harry." For the first time, units representing organized labor marched in the inaugural parade with their own floats. On orders from the White

HOW TRUMAN DEFEATED DEWEY IN 1948

In the election of 1948 Truman received 24.1 million votes—less than half the total popular vote but enough to win 28 states (below) having a total of 303 electoral votes. Dewey received 21.9 million votes, carrying 16 states with 189 electoral votes. The Dixiecrat party, which amassed 1.2 million votes, won four Southern states with 38 electoral votes (plus one ballot from a Tennessee elector who violated his Truman pledge) and also did well in Arkansas and Georgia. The Progressive party won no electoral votes; of its 1.2 million popular votes, New York cast 509,559.

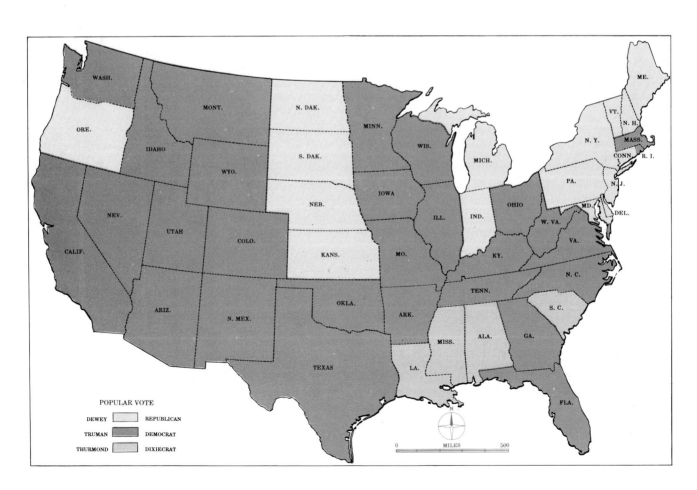

POPULAR VOTE

DEWEY	REPUBLICAN
TRUMAN	DEMOCRAT
THURMOND	DIXIECRAT

House, Negroes attended the inaugural gala and danced at the inaugural ball.

A British magazine entitled its postelection commentary: "Roosevelt's Fifth Term." Truman's State of the Union message indicated that the title was appropriate. As part of his "Fair Deal" program he called for the extension of old Roosevelt measures, such as social security, and added such new proposals as a national plan for compulsory health insurance.

Congress in 1949 expanded public power, soil conservation, flood control and rural electrification programs, and granted the President powers to cope with inflation. It provided for the construction of low-income housing units, and made grants for slum clearance and rural housing. It also voted a new and somewhat liberalized Displaced Persons Act. But Congress refused to heed Truman's requests on most of the major issues of the day: It turned down fair-employment-practices legislation, Secretary of Agriculture Charles Brannan's new plan for farm subsidies, and the President's proposal for a national health program. Federal aid to education lost out when controversy developed over extending such aid to parochial schools.

On some issues, Truman found that he had to oppose action by the Democratic Congress. He courageously vetoed a bill which would have raised the price of natural gas, even though the measure was supported by powerful elements in his own party.

By 1951 Truman and Congress had reached a stalemate. The President did not have enough support to win passage for his recommendations, and the conservatives were not strong enough to undo what had already been done. This was the same kind of stalemate that had characterized much of the country's legislative history since 1938, a politics of dead center.

But the country had been led through the difficult postwar transition—and by a man who, as one writer noted, was "not so much the average man as he is the national character in office." Under Truman America had forged a coalition of free nations in the Atlantic community, had made a start toward a development program for the Asian and African nations, had turned back the tide of Communism threatening Western Europe, had broken new ground in the relations of white and Negro Americans, and had made the difficult shift from a wartime to a peacetime economy without a serious depression.

A figure familiar to troops overseas, Francis Cardinal Spellman, archbishop of New York and Roman Catholic Military Vicar of the Armed Forces, visited units all over the world. At home, he often took stands on public issues. He urged, for example, that U.S. immigration restrictions be relaxed to admit the "starving, suffering peoples" who were displaced by war.

NONE of these advances had come easily. One analyst wrote: "Mr. Truman had to make many choices in situations in which there was no right way, but only an assortment of wrong ones. . . . It takes uncommon steadiness of mind to commit a nation to a choice between evils and having made the choice, neither to misrepresent it nor to wallow in regrets and unnerving doubts. If any one thing seems more nearly certain than another about Harry Truman as President, it is that he never shrank from a necessary choice."

Despite his extensive reading in history, Truman retained a simple, straightforward view of the world derived from a Missouri boyhood. "A man brought up in this tradition," Jonathan Daniels noted, "does not get bogged down in a political campaign or a cold war because of inner uncertainties or ideological complications. A Bolshevik is as simple as a bushwhacker." Sometimes this led the President to superficial judgments based on overly simple, unreflective views of complex subjects. But it freed him to make bold decisions, and he never flinched from those decisions. Perhaps the best clue to his actions was a sign on his White House desk: "The buck ends here."

ANTICOMMUNISTS in Leslie, Michigan (population 1,400), line up with a scroll bearing over 900 signatures. The document endorsed Judge Harold Medina's conduct of the 1949 trial in which 11 Communists were convicted of promoting subversive ideas.

Bitter years of fear and distrust

AMERICANS found little respite in the victory that crowned World War II. In place of the old enemy, Nazism, there was a new one, Communism; and it suddenly seemed to have planted itself everywhere. In a dark kaleidoscope of espionage and subversion, frightening disclosures were made by former Communists Elizabeth Bentley, Louis Budenz and Whittaker Chambers. Among those indicted were ex-government official Alger Hiss and a couple named Julius and Ethel Rosenberg, who passed defense secrets to Russia.

The first major loyalty trial, held in 1949, set a hectic pattern of sensational charges and countercharges. Eleven Communist leaders were convicted, not of committing subversive acts, but of advocating the forcible overthrow of the government. Before the defendants went to prison, their attorneys had angered Americans (above) with their violent abuse of the presiding judge. The next year saw the rise to power of Senator Joseph R. McCarthy, whose name became symbolic of the excesses of the whole period. But McCarthy himself finally alienated the public with his reckless attacks. The 1954 Army-McCarthy hearings (opposite) signaled the end of the senator's sway—and the end of enervating public suspicions and private anxieties. Eventually, there proved to be far less Communist infiltration than many believed, and the investigations did far less damage to civil liberties than many feared. But the wounds that were opened in those few years would be slow to heal.

THE CLIMAX OF McCARTHYISM is reached under glaring TV lights at the Army-McCarthy hearings in the Senate Caucus Room in 1954. Backs to the camera, Senators Mundt (right) and McClellan face Army Secretary Robert T. Stevens (center). Stevens is flanked by his counsel, Joseph N. Welch (right), and the departmental counselor of the Army, John G. Adams.

THE ACCUSER, Richard M. Nixon, takes notes at a Hiss hearing. The most tenacious of the committee members, Nixon insisted upon the personal confrontation of Hiss and Chambers.

Hiss vs. Chambers:
"A generation on trial"

MORE than the guilt or innocence of Alger Hiss was at stake when this former government official stood accused—in 1948 House hearings and later in court—of passing secret documents to Russia via ex-Communist courier Whittaker Chambers. Experts swore that these papers could have let Russia break State Department codes. The Hiss case, and treason charges against other trusted men at home and abroad, added up, said journalist Alistair Cooke, to "a generation on trial."

Chambers produced not only the documents, which had apparently been copied on Hiss's old Woodstock typewriter, but also summaries of secret papers in Hiss's handwriting. Other testimony produced at the trial linked Hiss to members of the Communist underground. He was found guilty of perjury and sentenced to prison.

THE ACCUSED, Alger Hiss, takes his oath before the House Un-American Activities Committee. He testified that in substance Chambers' charges against him were "complete fabrications."

THE WITNESS, Whittaker Chambers, takes the stand at a committee hearing. "I had myself served in the underground," he said quietly; "a member of this group . . . was Alger Hiss."

COMMITTEE MEMBERS ponder the conflicting stories of Hiss and Chambers. They are, from left, Karl Mundt of South Dakota, Chairman J. Parnell Thomas of New Jersey, F. Edward Hébert of Louisiana, Richard B. Vail of Illinois. Before Hiss was convicted, Thomas was imprisoned—for padding his payroll.

A wave of hearings that engulfed a nation

Few Americans were wholly unaffected by the wave of security investigations. Public-opinion polls, widespread suspicions and fears for civil liberties reflected the strain under which the country was laboring.

Among the countless citizens whose loyalty was impugned were the four below. Annie Lee Moss, a Pentagon clerk, was denounced in 1954 before the McCarthy committee; a year later the Army gave her back a job. Owen Lattimore, a minor Far Eastern policy adviser, was called by McCarthy the "top Russian espionage agent" in America; none of the charges against him ever came to trial. Screen writer Dalton Trumbo did go to jail in 1950 as one of the "Hollywood Ten" who refused to answer the questions of congressmen. In 1953 Methodist bishop G. Bromley Oxnam asked to testify, and for 10 hours he refuted unsubstantiated slurs against him. In the end he was given a clean bill of health.

Clerk Annie Lee Moss   *Professor Owen Lattimore*

Bishop G. Bromley Oxnam   *Writer Dalton Trumbo*

A FRIENDLY WITNESS, actor Robert Taylor, leaves a House hearing in October of 1947. With Gary Cooper and others, Taylor indicated that Communists were at work in Hollywood.

FOUR UNDER FIRE in the hearings are shown opposite. Although many government employees were investigated as "security risks," not one was formally charged with sedition.

UNFRIENDLY DEMONSTRATORS march in Detroit in 1952. People of all shades of political conviction protested the investigations as a clear infringement on the Bill of Rights.

51

Joe McCarthy's downfall: "What did I do wrong?"

ARLY in 1954 Senator Joe McCarthy was riding high. To be sure, his no-holds-barred tactics had made powerful enemies. But few dared to challenge him.

Having cowed the State Department, McCarthy took on the Army in the spring of 1954. For 36 days the Army-McCarthy hearings kept Americans close to their TV sets. The Army's chief counsel was a Massachusetts lawyer, Joseph N. Welch (below), who at first seemed too mild to cope with McCarthy's slashing forays. But when the senator attacked Welch's young assistant, Welch made a moving defense—and the hearing room burst into applause. In retrospect, many observers have dated McCarthy's decline from that dramatic moment.

"What did I do wrong?" asked McCarthy afterward. He never recovered. His Senate colleagues voted to "condemn" him. Worse, the newspapers ceased giving him headlines. His friends saw him deteriorate physically. When he died in 1957, Dean Acheson was asked to make a comment. McCarthy's archenemy coldly quoted in Latin the maxim, "Speak nothing but good of the dead."

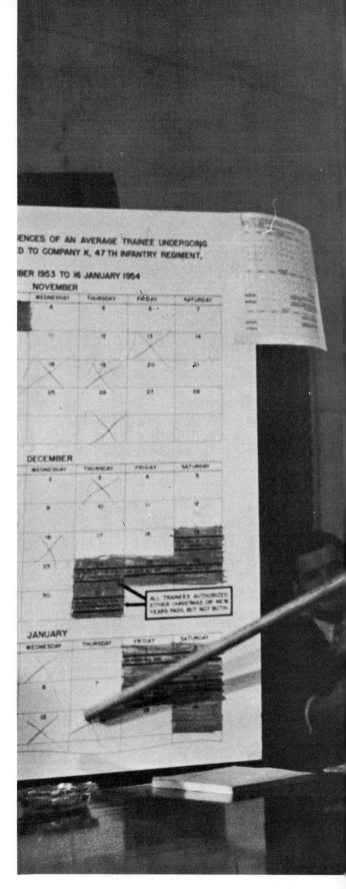

DEFENDING THE ARMY, Joseph Welch speaks up at the 1954 Army-McCarthy hearings. He later said America was protected from demagogues by "immense reservoirs of common sense."

ATTACKING THE ARMY, Joe McCarthy wields a pointer as Roy M. Cohn, McCarthy's subcommittee counsel, looks on. The charts were intended to show that the Army was unfair

52

in its treatment of Private G. David Schine, formerly an un-salaried investigator for the subcommittee. The Army charged that McCarthy and Cohn sought preferential treatment for Schine; McCarthy charged that the Army held Schine "hostage" to force him to call off his investigations. A few months after this hearing, McCarthy and McCarthyism were on the wane.

3. AN ERA OF BAD FEELING

IN the years after World War II, America's deep involvement in foreign affairs confounded the nation's critics and astonished its admirers. Yet this change from prewar isolationism was by no means so complete as it sometimes appeared. Many of the die-hard isolationists maintained an outlook based on some of the old assumptions: America's great strength freed it to act unilaterally in foreign affairs; America had a unique moral mission; Europe was not to be trusted. This group found much that was objectionable in United States foreign policy. They were particularly exasperated by a strategy of containment premised on the belief that the United States had to live with the danger of world Communism indefinitely.

Those Republicans who clung to isolationism found the postwar world especially vexing. Sincerely convinced that their way was best for the country, they were stunned by Harry S. Truman's 1948 victory. But even as the Democrats celebrated their triumph, the country was witnessing the first of a series of events which would persuade millions of Americans that subversive influences were to blame for upsetting the comfortable old order and for jeopardizing the nation's security. These developments—the Hiss trial, the fall of China, the advent of McCarthyism and warfare in Korea—would detonate an explosion of ill feeling that would shatter the Democratic coalition and bring the Republicans to power for the first time in 20 years.

Three months before the election of 1948, a stocky, carelessly dressed

AT WAR IN KOREA, American troops keep a deadly vigil in 1951, bearing the brunt of the United Nations' three-year struggle to restore peace to that ravaged peninsula.

magazine editor named Whittaker Chambers came before the House Committee on Un-American Activities. Chambers, an admitted former Communist, said that Alger Hiss, a former State Department official and now head of the Carnegie Endowment for International Peace, had been a longtime member of the Communist party. Hiss sued Chambers for libel. Chambers rested on his word, and Truman dismissed the affair as a "red herring" designed by the committee to distract attention from the failures of the 80th Congress.

Then on a December night in 1948, Chambers led two investigators to a pumpkin patch on his farm. He reached into one pumpkin and pulled out microfilm of classified State Department documents, which he swore had been passed on to him by a spy ring of which Hiss was a member. Now it was no longer a question of party membership; Chambers was accusing Hiss of having been a spy. On December 15, 1948, a grand jury indicted Hiss for perjury. The statute of limitations barred the indictment of Hiss for espionage, but everyone understood that treason was the real issue.

The Hiss case captured the attention of the nation. At first, Chambers seemed to have the worst of it. A confessed former spy was not a man whose word necessarily commanded belief. But when he was asked why he testified against Hiss, Chambers responded: "I do not hate Mr. Hiss. We were close friends, but we are caught in a tragedy of history. Mr. Hiss represents the concealed enemy against which we are all fighting, and I am fighting. I have testified against him with remorse and pity, but in a moment of history in which this Nation now stands, so help me God, I could not do otherwise."

The verdict in Hiss's first trial reflected the country's uncertainty: The hung jury voted 8 to 4 for conviction. In November 1949 Hiss stood trial a second time. As the months went by, even some Hiss partisans began to sense that the weight of evidence suggested he was not telling the truth. In January 1950 the jury found Hiss guilty, and he was sentenced to five years in jail.

F OR frustrated Republicans seeking an issue to return them to power, Hiss was a godsend. The charge had been raised that the country's lost security was the result of subversion. A sensational spy trial in Canada in 1946 had uncovered at least 14 government employees who had turned over secrets to foreign agents; several of the spy rings had operated in the United States. But the Hiss case had special aspects which made it almost as important for American history as the Dreyfus affair was for France at the turn of the century.

Hiss seemed a perfect symbol of the Roosevelt-Truman foreign policy. He had been director of the Office of Special Political Affairs in the State Department; he had served as executive secretary at the San Francisco Conference; he had been present—in an insignificant role—at Yalta. He represented all that the Midwestern Republicans distrusted: Harvard, the Atlantic Seaboard, the New Deal—all the forces of internationalism and social change that had been altering the familiar contours of the nation.

If the symbol of Hiss was lacking in any respect, it was in its irrelevance to the foreign policy of President Truman and his Secretary of State, Dean Acheson. The Chambers revelations dealt with events of the '30s, and Hiss had resigned from the State Department two years before Acheson became Secretary. It was the Secretary himself—natty, stiff-backed, with a bristling British-style mustache—who made the symbol complete. Senator Hugh Butler of Nebraska expostulated: "I look at that fellow, I watch his smart-aleck

"McCarthyism" became a household word shortly after it was coined in this 1950 Herblock cartoon. McCarthy's tactics as chief inquisitor of alleged Communists and subversives intimidated many officials. When Senator Margaret Chase Smith of Maine challenged McCarthy with her "Declaration of Conscience," only six Republican colleagues dared to support her.

manner and his British clothes and that New Dealism, everlasting New Dealism in everything he says and does, and I want to shout, Get out, Get out. You stand for everything that has been wrong with the United States for years."

Four days after Hiss was convicted, Acheson, who had known Hiss for years, said in a press conference: "I do not intend to turn my back on Alger Hiss." Many felt that Acheson's statement did him credit as a man; nevertheless it was politically maladroit. Once again the Truman Administration was accused of indifference to treason. The accusation was unwarranted. Truman had initiated a program to oust subversives from government. By 1951 some 212 employees had been fired and 2,000 had resigned. Many people objected that the program was far too rigorous, and Truman himself came to share these opinions.

In the field of foreign policy the main grievance of many Administration critics seemed to be that the United States was much too closely involved with Europe and that too little attention was being paid to Asian affairs. Moreover, they recognized that it was in the Orient that the Democratic performance in foreign affairs was most vulnerable.

The United States had long regarded itself as a special friend of China. But during and after World War II, China was torn by internal strife between Communists led by Mao Tse-tung and the Kuomintang government of Chiang Kai-shek. During the war Ambassador Patrick J. Hurley had pressed Chiang to form a coalition government with the Communists, but Chiang refused. In December 1945 President Truman sent General George Marshall to China to try, if possible, to create just such a coalition. In January 1947 he returned, unable to effect this unrealistic agreement, and critical of both sides.

The smoldering civil war then erupted, and the Communists demonstrated their military superiority. Supporters of Chiang urged Truman to speed aid to him. The President was willing to give limited assistance—more than three billion dollars in grants and credits and one billion dollars in war materials sold at bargain-basement prices—but he would not make a massive commitment in China of the sort he was making in Europe, largely because he and his advisers doubted that Chiang could be saved unless troops were sent.

On August 5, 1949, the State Department announced the jolting news that China had fallen to the Reds. "The government and the Kuomintang," Acheson declared, ". . . had sunk into corruption . . . and into reliance on the United States to win the war for them." For the United States to have saved Chiang, he argued, would have required "full-scale intervention in behalf of a government which had lost the confidence of its own troops and its own people."

Critics of the Democrats' foreign policy insisted that China had been lost not because of Chiang's weakness but largely because of vacillation or subversion in the government. The conservative columnist George Sokolsky claimed: "The errors which brought on his defeat were not Chiang's; they were Marshall's. They were not China's; they were America's."

THERE is no question that the Roosevelt-Truman policy in China was open to criticism. The Chinese Communists had persistently been described as benign agrarian reformers. (Some conservatives, too, had underestimated the despotic character of the Reds. General Hurley, who had been ambassador to China, had once compared them to "Oklahoma Republicans," though he later changed his mind.) Critics also pointed out that the new State Department position on Chiang was in direct contradiction to the previous position

As China fell to the Communists, America's fear of Marxism reached a hysterical pitch. The scapegoat was Secretary of State Dean Acheson (above). The New York "News" predicted that Acheson would "enter the oblivion which he has so well and truly earned." Even Walter Lippmann advised Acheson's retirement. But Truman said tersely, "I refuse to dismiss Acheson."

Georgi Malenkov, secretary of the Soviet Central Committee, is pictured here as "Stalin's Stooge." Once described as "sinister" and "repulsive," Malenkov had a keen sense of political balance. He survived many purges and in 1946 preached a bold new idea that later became gospel: Marx just might not have foreseen every problem; experience might supply answers.

that he was a powerful ally who led one of the world's four great powers. The Administration, they claimed, had never given Chiang aid commensurate with that status. Nor had it prepared the United States for the China disaster.

However it seems unlikely that any action short of massive military intervention could have defeated the Chinese Reds—and responsible officials were convinced that Americans would never have tolerated any such move. In any event, Administration supporters insisted, the view that a half billion Asians had been sold out by a few American functionaries betrayed an unjustifiable belief in the omnipotence of the United States. Dean Acheson insisted that "Nothing that [America] did or could have done within the reasonable limits of its capabilities could have changed that result."

IN September 1949, only a few weeks after Chiang's collapse, reporters were called to the White House to hear more bad news. "Close the doors," ordered the President's press secretary. "Nobody is leaving here until everybody has this statement." The first reporter who read the terse announcement on the press handout let out a startled whistle. It read: "We have evidence that within recent weeks an atomic explosion occurred in the U.S.S.R."

Russia had The Bomb, at least three years ahead of the schedule American scientists had predicted. No doubt the United States had underestimated Soviet technical ability. But to some Americans another explanation suggested itself. "It now appears," said G.O.P. Senator Karl Mundt of South Dakota, "that earlier and prevailing laxity in safeguarding this country against Communist espionage has permitted what were once the secrets of our atomic bomb to fall into the hands of America's only potential enemy."

The threat of nuclear devastation now seemed immensely greater. "There is only one thing worse than one nation having the atomic bomb," said Nobel Prize winner Harold Urey, "—that's two nations having it." When in January 1950 Truman announced that America was working on the even deadlier hydrogen bomb, Albert Einstein warned: "General annihilation beckons."

Some of the mystery surrounding Russian acquisition of the A-bomb was ended in February 1950 when the British announced they had arrested Klaus Fuchs, an atomic scientist who had worked at Los Alamos. Fuchs confessed that from mid-1942 to early in 1949 he had turned over valuable scientific secrets to Soviet agents—enough, it was estimated, to speed up Soviet production of the A-bomb "at least a year." (Fuchs's confession was later to lead to the trial, conviction and ultimate execution for espionage of Americans Julius and Ethel Rosenberg, who were named as major accomplices.)

"How much more are we going to have to take?" fumed Republican Senator Homer Capehart on the Senate floor. "Fuchs and Acheson and Hiss and hydrogen bombs threatening outside and New Dealism eating away the vitals of the nation. In the name of Heaven, is this the best America can do?"

One man with a sense of the historic moment had a ready answer for Capehart's question. Still unknown to most of the country, he was in a few weeks' time to give his name to a brief, brutal era of American history. He was the junior senator from Wisconsin, Joseph R. McCarthy.

On February 9, 1950, two weeks after Hiss was sentenced to jail, McCarthy addressed a Republican meeting in Wheeling, West Virginia. The speech seemed of so little importance at the time that there is no authenticated transcript of McCarthy's remarks, but newsmen recalled his saying: "I have here in my hand a list of 205—a list of names that were known to the Secretary of State as being members of the Communist party and who nevertheless are still working and shaping the policy in the State Department." Most of the national press overlooked the Wheeling speech. The next day in Salt Lake City McCarthy made similar charges, and the following day he hit the same theme in Reno. By now the accusations were beginning to make headlines.

In a long address on March 30, McCarthy shifted his attack to focus on the Orient. He stigmatized Professor Owen Lattimore, a longtime student of Far Eastern affairs, as "the top Russian espionage agent." The fact is that however unsound Lattimore's judgment may have been, no substantial evidence was ever submitted that the Johns Hopkins professor was a spy; furthermore the State Department under Truman had rarely consulted Lattimore and had not followed his advice when it did.

McCarthy did not pause to answer refutations; he moved from sensation to sensation, ruining one career after another with unsupported accusations. Senators in both parties were troubled by his rashness. An investigating committee headed by Democratic Senator Millard Tydings of Maryland issued a majority report which ridiculed the substance of the Wisconsin senator's charges and denounced his methods. Unhappily, this report failed to make a judicious appraisal of the charges and thus added fuel to McCarthy's fire.

More impressive was a manifesto issued by seven G.O.P. senators—Margaret Chase Smith of Maine, Irving Ives of New York, Charles Tobey of New Hampshire, George Aiken of Vermont, Wayne Morse of Oregon, Edward Thye of Minnesota and Robert Hendrickson of New Jersey. In their "Declaration of Conscience," they dissociated themselves from "Certain elements of the Republican Party [who] have materially added to this confusion in the hopes of riding the Republican Party to victory through the selfish political exploitation of fear, bigotry, ignorance, and intolerance."

But a much larger number of G.O.P. senators—as well as many Southern Democrats—believed that McCarthy was right. Robert Taft was heard to remark: "McCarthy should keep talking, and if one case doesn't work out he should proceed with another." Taft said he had meant merely that McCarthy should not be muzzled; others interpreted the statement as a hunting license.

By September 1950, little more than six months after McCarthy's Wheeling speech, concern over subversion appeared to have conquered good sense. Monogram Pictures canceled plans for a movie on Longfellow because Hiawatha had tried to bring peace to the Indians, and the film might be construed as support for a Soviet "peace offensive." That same month the Senate, overriding Truman's veto, adopted the Internal Security Act, which placed stringent restrictions on Communist activities, provided for the detention of dangerous subversives in time of emergency and set up a Subversive Activities Control Board. Although the bill jeopardized civil liberties by curtailing freedom of speech, some distinguished liberals in the Senate voted for it; one senator confessed privately that he had done so out of fear of McCarthyism.

In linking anxiety over subversion to Truman's Far Eastern policy, McCarthy had struck gold. He pushed his assault further beyond the bounds of reason. "It was Moscow," he charged, ". . . which decreed that the United States should execute its loyal friend, the Republic of China. The executioners were that well-defined group headed by Acheson and George Catlett Marshall."

A FAKE PICTURE GETS
READ INTO THE RECORD

Public dread of anything linked to Communism was a powerful weapon in the hands of unscrupulous politicians. One noted victim was Senator Millard Tydings of Maryland. His opponent, John Marshall Butler, used the top picture above (of Tydings listening to election returns in 1938) and the reversed middle picture (American Communist leader Earl Browder in 1950) and published the composite (bottom) in a circular. Although the caption mentioned that it was a composite, the defeated Tydings sadly noted that "one picture is worth a thousand words."

"Like animal trainers . . . ready to show off a monster," the Atomic Energy Commission in 1952 held its first open-to-the-press atomic blast. Some guests, like Senators Margaret Chase Smith, Leverett Saltonstall and Lyndon Johnson (above), chose to watch it on television, but 200 notables were 10 miles from Ground Zero. Happily the bombardier's aim was perfect.

The State Department viewed criticism of its Far Eastern policy with no little complacency. It took pride in the fact that America's occupation policy, directed by General Douglas MacArthur, had converted its former totalitarian enemy, Japan, into a valuable democratic ally. And Japan, the planners were convinced, was the key to power in the Orient. "I am sure," George Kennan commented, "that the Russians would gladly exchange our control of Japan for their control of China." But when the State Department came to grief in the Orient, it was not over China or Japan—at least directly—but over a country to which few Americans had ever given any thought.

In the closing days of World War II, the United States had hastily proposed to accept the surrender of Japanese troops in Korea south of the 38th Parallel; the forces of the U.S.S.R. would have similar authority north of the parallel. This accommodation turned out to be temporarily advantageous for the United States because Russian troops had raced down the peninsula before the Americans landed. When the Americans arrived, the Soviets obligingly gave up the capital of Seoul and retired north of the parallel.

Within a brief period, however, the United States and Soviet Russia were deeply divided over the future of Korea. North of the 38th Parallel the Soviet Union fostered a Communist government. To the south, Dr. Syngman Rhee formed a Western-oriented republic under U.N. sponsorship and, for the moment, under the military protection of the United States.

For America, Korea posed a thorny political and military problem. Among others, General Charles G. Helmick, former Deputy Military Governor of Korea, had warned that the peninsula was indefensible. Truman favored a sharp cutback in military spending, and Republicans in Congress opposed sending aid. Although Lieutenant General John R. Hodge, commanding United States forces in Korea, warned that if the Americans pulled out, the Communists would take over, Washington proposed a withdrawal of both Soviet and American troops. In January 1949 the U.S.S.R. pulled out its forces; six months later the United States followed suit. However the Russians left the North Koreans heavily armed. The United States, on the other hand, in part out of fear that Rhee might mount an invasion northward, gave the Republic of Korea only modest military training and equipment.

On January 12, 1950, Secretary Acheson outlined a "defensive perimeter" which defined the limits of the area the United States believed vital to its national security. Both Korea and Formosa lay outside this perimeter. Acheson's statement did not preclude the possibility that the United States would fight if the Republic of Korea were attacked, but it suggested that Korea was by no means viewed as vital to America's national interest.

ON June 25, 1950, only five months after Acheson's address, North Korean forces invaded the Republic of Korea. The next day the United States took the question to the U.N. Security Council. The Council—in the absence of the U.S.S.R., which was boycotting sessions in an effort to oust Nationalist China—ordered the North Koreans to withdraw and then called upon U.N. members to come to the aid of the Republic of Korea.

That day Truman flew to Washington from Independence, Missouri, where he had been visiting his family. During the trip he "recalled some earlier instances: Manchuria, Ethiopia, Austria . . . how each time that the democracies failed to act it had encouraged the aggressors to keep going ahead. . . .

If this was allowed to go unchallenged, it would mean a third world war."

When General MacArthur reported that the collapse of South Korea was imminent, Truman ordered American air and naval power to the aid of the republic. Later, on MacArthur's advice, the President authorized the use of American ground troops. Truman stipulated that the intervention in Korea would be limited and that in no respect was it to be conceived as a war either with the U.S.S.R. or with Red China. He was equally intent on avoiding the spread of the conflict to the mainland. He sent the Seventh Fleet to serve as a barrier between Formosa and the Chinese mainland, an action which, in effect, contained the war. In the United States this action drew criticism from those who wanted to encourage Chiang to invade the continent.

THE intervention in Korea received the backing of most Americans; Henry Wallace approved, and so did Senator Kenneth Wherry of Nebraska, one of the most powerful of the isolationists. The U.N. swiftly endorsed America's actions and authorized the United States to assume command of U.N. troops in Korea. For the first time in the history of man, a world organization had mobilized force to halt aggression. But since the United States provided a disproportionate share of the troops, the U.N. intervention seemed to most Americans to be simply a United States engagement. (In the end, the United States supplied roughly 33 per cent of the U.N. forces; the Republic of Korea, 61 per cent; other nations, less than 6 per cent.)

In terms of immediately available troops, the Korean War caught America ill prepared. General MacArthur, named to command the U.N. forces, could for the moment draw on only four undertrained, poorly equipped occupation divisions in Japan; in reserve in the States he had only one Army division and part of a Marine division. He had no choice save to throw his green troops into the battle in the hope that their sacrifice would permit him to stabilize a defense line. The Republic of Korea forces were in full flight and might be driven into the sea. To prevent a disaster, soldiers of the 24th Division headed by Major General William Dean were hurried to Korea from Japan.

The GIs disembarked at the southeastern port of Pusan to a welcome with bands and banners. One soldier, perhaps boasting to cover the insecurity so many troopers felt, said, "Just wait till the gooks see an American uniform—they'll turn around and run like hell!" It took only one engagement to make a mockery of these words. The North Koreans, equipped with heavy Russian-made T-34 tanks, rolled through the American lines. In this first encounter the Americans had not a single tank, nor antitank mine, nor armor-penetrating bazooka. On July 8 General Dean informed MacArthur: "I am convinced that the North Korean Army...[has been] underestimated."

The summer of 1950 was a bitter season. Not since the Civil War had the percentage of casualties among high-ranking officers of a U.S. army been so great. Outfought and outnumbered, the American soldiers sloshed through the steaming rice paddies in a disorderly retreat. General Dean was captured. American GIs were found lying in ditches with their hands bound behind their backs and bullet holes in their heads. The U.N. forces were driven all the way back to a small perimeter around Pusan. In six weeks the Americans had suffered 6,000 casualties, the South Korean forces 70,000.

But at the Pusan perimeter the Americans held. By September the North Koreans had been repulsed by fresh troops from the United States.

Japan's Emperor Hirohito was once considered a descendant of the gods upon whom no ordinary mortal might gaze. But a month after the occupation of Japan began, he made a precedent-shattering call on Supreme Commander MacArthur at the American embassy. This picture of their meeting was convincing proof to the Japanese that the old order had passed.

"Those are the flags of various gangster mobs and millionaires. Now shut up."   AUG. '50

Early in the Korean War, Warren Austin, U.S. ambassador to the U.N., said Russia was "assisting . . . the invaders"—and a top Soviet official admitted the North Koreans were using Soviet army equipment. In this Herblock cartoon a Russian officer scolds a North Korean soldier gazing apprehensively at the banners of the U.N. forces gathering against him.

Now that the enemy had been halted, the U.N. forces were ready to take the initiative. MacArthur decided on a bold tactic: to launch an amphibious assault far behind the North Korean lines at Inchon. "We shall land at Inchon," the general insisted, "and I shall crush them." And so he did. To carry out his brilliant scheme, MacArthur created the X Corps out of Army and Marine units. Early in the morning of September 15, Marines landed on Wolmi, the island which protected Inchon harbor. Taken completely by surprise, the North Koreans offered little resistance to the capture of Inchon. After some nasty fighting, Seoul, too, fell to the X Corps in late September.

In the southeast the Eighth Army stormed out of the Pusan perimeter and raced north, sometimes covering 30 miles a day. By the end of September the North Korean army had been shattered. Very few of those who had headed south across the parallel in June lived to recross it that fall. The triumph at Inchon had brought U.N. forces to the 38th Parallel by early October.

THE rapid change of fortunes confronted the United States and the U.N. with a crucial decision. Exponents of containment argued that since the North Korean invasion had been repulsed, the U.N. had achieved its objective; it should consolidate its lines on the 38th Parallel and negotiate a settlement. But MacArthur was eager to pursue the remnants of the North Korean army northward with the aim of preventing the enemy from regrouping; his larger purpose was to unite the peninsula.

Despite the grave risk that China might intervene, the Administration decided to abandon the containment policy in this instance. The Joint Chiefs ordered MacArthur to achieve "the destruction of the North Korean Armed Forces" and authorized him to cross the parallel. On October 7, 1950, the United Nations General Assembly endorsed the plan. A week later President Truman conferred with General MacArthur on Wake Island. Accounts of what took place vary widely, but on the basis of what MacArthur told him, Truman approved an advance to within a few miles of the Chinese border. Enemy resistance, MacArthur predicted, would be ended by Thanksgiving.

For several weeks it seemed that MacArthur's optimism was justified. The U.N. advance into North Korea gained steadily. On October 19 the North Korean capital of Pyongyang fell, and parachutists landing about 30 miles beyond trapped half of the North Korean army.

But on October 26 came a disquieting event: the capture of a Chinese Communist soldier. On November 1 Chinese troops badly cut up the 8th Regiment of the U.S. 1st Cavalry; it was, a spokesman reported, "a massacre like the one which hit Custer." Although the fact was still undetected by American intelligence, this isolated incident showed that the Chinese were ready to fight in full force; the gamble that China would not intervene had been lost.

The Chinese assault on the U.S. 1st Cavalry took place in the final week of political campaigning in America's midterm elections of 1950. After the Inchon victory, Democrats hoped to ride the crest of national pride in a triumphant war. But the Korean conflict was never a popular war, and the country was dismayed by its cost. By November 3, Election Day, casualties had reached 28,235, and these did not include dead, wounded and missing in the Chinese offensive. When the nation went to the polls, the newspapers were black with the unnerving news of the assault by Mao's troops.

In the election the Republicans picked up 28 seats in the House and five in the Senate. The gains were modest (the smallest in the House in an off-year election since 1934), and they left the Democrats still nominally in control, although by a narrow margin, in both houses. But the setback to Truman was more decisive than the figures indicated. A number of Administration supporters were ousted, including Senate Majority Leader Scott Lucas of Illinois and Majority Whip Francis Myers of Pennsylvania. A widely remarked feature of the elections was the power of what was now generally referred to as "McCarthyism." The Wisconsin senator received more invitations from G.O.P. candidates to speak in their states than all other senators combined, and he was credited with playing a part in the defeat of a number of Democrats. In Utah, Senator Elbert Thomas was ousted after 18 years in the Senate, in a campaign in which he was charged with being soft on Communism.

In California Congressman Richard M. Nixon exploited the McCarthyite issues to win a Senate seat from his Democratic opponent, Congresswoman Helen Gahagan Douglas. Nixon, who had first captured attention through his dogged pursuit of Alger Hiss in the House Un-American Activities Committee, linked Mrs. Douglas, as a former actress and the wife of Hollywood star Melvyn Douglas, to suspicions of Communist infiltration of the movie capital.

The main consequence of the 1950 elections was to fortify the opponents of Administration foreign policy. Shortly after the elections, heartened by their gains and no longer restrained by the ailing Senator Vandenberg, these critics began a "great debate" in the Senate on foreign affairs. Led by Senator Taft, they called for a re-examination of America's military and foreign policies and questioned whether the defense of Western Europe was vital to America's security.

Above all, Taft feared that obligations abroad might bankrupt America and lead to the destruction of the American system. "We cannot assume a financial burden in our foreign policy so great that it threatens liberty at home," Taft insisted. He found a strong supporter in Herbert Hoover, who argued that until Europe manned its own defenses, the United States should retreat to its own side of the Atlantic. "The foundation of our national policies," Hoover stated, "must be to preserve for the world this Western Hemisphere Gibraltar of Western civilization." In mid-February 1951 a majority of House Republicans endorsed Hoover's proposals. Not until April 4, 1951, did the Senate approve the sending of four additional divisions to Europe to fulfill American NATO commitments, and even then it advised the President to send no more troops to Western Europe without congressional authorization.

While Administration adversaries opposed a strong policy in Europe, they continued to favor a bold policy in Asia. They had no patience with the conception of "limited war," which they felt implied that America could not defeat its enemies. Much of the country shared this impatience. As one writer observed: "Because Americans for the first time lived in a world in which they could not truly win, whatever the effort, and from which they could not withdraw, without disaster, for millions the result was trauma."

A COUNTRY taught by its history to believe in the quick, total solution, the United States had to unlearn its past. But no nation surrenders the lessons of its past easily, least of all a nation with so happy a history. The consequence of America's reluctance to change was a period of bad feeling that Americans were soon to look back upon with shame and remorse.

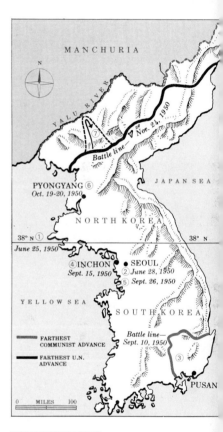

THE KOREAN WAR:
JUNE-NOVEMBER 1950

As shown above, both sides made their deepest penetration early in the Korean War. After crossing the 38th Parallel (1), the North Koreans quickly took Seoul (2), South Korea's capital. United Nations troops were driven south as far as the defense line shown around Pusan (3). Then the U.N.'s amphibious attack at Inchon (4) turned the tide. U.N. units recaptured Seoul (5) and seized Pyongyang (6), capital of North Korea. Patrols reached the Yalu River (7) as the U.N. advance neared high tide. But the U.N. forces had blundered into a trap (map, page 79).

A savage war for world security

THE Korean War began at 4 a.m. on June 25, 1950, when the People's Democratic Republic of Korea (North Korea), performing on strings pulled by Moscow, executed a carefully planned attack on the Republic of Korea (South Korea) across the 38th Parallel, which had divided the country since the end of World War II. On July 27, 1953, the conflict drew to an uneasy close along the same boundary, almost exactly where it had started. An armistice was signed at Panmunjom by an American general representing the United Nations and a Russian-born Korean general representing the North Korean People's Army and the Chinese Communist forces.

During the more than three years of fierce fighting, the tide of battle raged back and forth across the jumbled mountains and rough valleys of that inhospitable peninsula *(map, page 63)*. Seoul, the capital of South Korea, changed hands four times. Some two million servicemen from 18 countries were killed or wounded fighting for tracts of primitive wilderness. But issues of transcendent importance were at stake in Korea. The original invasion had been a Communist challenge—a blatant defiance of the United Nations. For the first time in history, a world community of nations had voted *(above)* to take arms "to repel . . . armed attack and to restore international peace and security." And the United States, in assuming the main burden of the U.N.'s commitment, had made it inescapably clear to the Communist powers that Americans were willing to fight and to die to resist aggression in faraway lands.

A RIPPLE OF ROCKETS rises over the central Korean front, as American Marines help to repel a Communist offensive in 1951. The rockets' blast revealed the position of the battery, and moments after the photograph was taken, the Marines had to pull out to escape return fire. The rockets, and most of the weapons used in Korea, were of World War II vintage.

GRIMACING WITH PAIN, a wounded Marine is carried to the rear by South Koreans during the U.N.'s fierce fight to hold the Pusan perimeter.

HURLING A GRENADE, a Marine rushes up to defend the crest of a hill against North Korean troops attacking from the next hill. This rain-drenched clash was part of U.N. efforts to expand the Pusan perimeter in September 1950.

Utter devastation is caught in an aerial photograph of the 1.5-million-barrel-a-year oil refinery at Wonsan inside North Korea. Despite

Mastery of the air—and a hectic, scrambling retreat

I<small>N</small> JUNE 1950, when the North Koreans drove south across the 38th Parallel, they expected to triumph in one swift stroke. Top American generals believed that such aggression "could be neutralized by air action."

On both sides the appraisals proved to be wrong. By July 10 the United Nations had destroyed North Korea's air force and had landed troops to slow the invasion. But the first U.N. units, Americans fresh from soft billets in Japan, were in poor shape for long, hard combat. Even worse, their training had conditioned them to fighting in a continuous battle line; they often panicked when separated by the enemy's deep thrusts. General Douglas MacArthur realized that the U.N.'s air supremacy meant little without enough infantry to hold the ground.

Through the terrible weeks of July the Americans alternately fought and fled, struggling to buy time for the U.N. buildup. Early in August they managed to set up a thin defense perimeter around the port of Pusan at the bottom of the peninsula. General Walton Walker told them: "There will be no more retreating, withdrawal, or ... anything else you want to call it." The U.N. troops finally had their continuous battle line, and they held.

CROSSING A RICE PADDY, American Marines dodge bursts of fire from enemy machine guns on the crests of nearby hills. Lying in their path is the body of a North Korean soldier.

overwhelming air superiority, which made it possible to inflict such heavy bomb damage, U.N. forces were almost driven into the sea.

ADVANCING BEHIND TANKS, U.N. troops enter a town near Pyongyang, capital of North Korea, in mid-October 1950. Only a month before, these units had been bottled up near Pusan.

Seizing the offensive with a daring seaborne strike

As new U.N. outfits arrived from America, General MacArthur planned to use some of them in a bold amphibious thrust at the enemy's rear areas. For his beachhead he selected Inchon, the seaport of Seoul. Many officers considered Inchon a foolhardy choice. To land there, the invaders would need both high tide and daylight, which coincided on just a few days a month. And Inchon's huge tides not only rose 30 feet but fell so fast that in 10 minutes boats could be marooned on broad mud flats under enemy guns.

Despite all obstacles, on September 15, 1950, the X Corps landed at Inchon (*left*) without a serious hitch. Overnight the U.N. position changed from the defense to the offense. Seoul, seized by the enemy on the fourth day of the war, was stormed and retaken. The Eighth Army broke out of its Pusan perimeter and linked up with the X Corps. Then both forces turned north in hot pursuit of the shattered North Korean Army. On every American's lips was the cry, "Home for Christmas!"

LANDING AT INCHON, Marines swarm from their boats at dusk on September 15, 1950. The invaders, stranded when the tide fell, had to secure their beachhead—or die there.

69

U.N. vehicles and civilians flee across the flats from Seoul as the victorious Chinese occupy the South Korean capital in January of 1951.

In North Korea, a swift advance, a shattering defeat

THE U.N. troops, excited by the success of their offensive, chased the enemy remnants north across the 38th Parallel. On November 24, 1950, General MacArthur confidently announced an attack which he believed would win the victory. But just four days later he reported: "This command . . . is now faced with conditions beyond its control and strength."

Two U.N. forces, rushing pell-mell toward the Manchurian border at the Yalu River, had run into a trap. Their scattered units were hit hard by some 300,000 Chinese "volunteers." Blowing bugles, the tough Chinese charged in great waves with utter disregard for their own losses. The U.N. troops resisted fiercely. In the freezing mountain passes around Changjin Reservoir, some 19,000 Marines and GIs held back up to 100,000 Chinese for several days. But in the end these troops had to fight a cruel retreat *(below and opposite)*, and all the U.N. units were driven south over ground they had paid dearly to take. Again, Americans had suffered a smashing defeat.

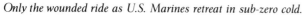

Only the wounded ride as U.S. Marines retreat in sub-zero cold.

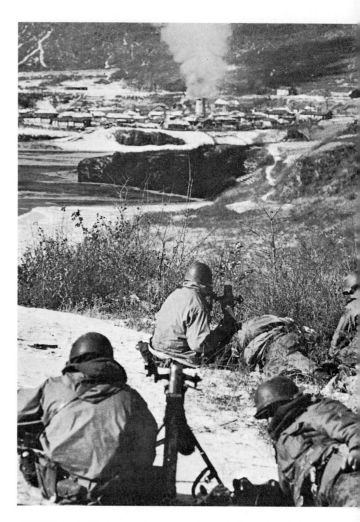

AT THE YALU, GIs fire mortars across the winding river boundary—and over Chinese territory—to hit Korean targets. They were repulsed in the Chinese onslaught of November 1950.

DOWN FROM THE MOUNTAINS, Marines retreat along the road known as "Nightmare Alley." Their group suffered 7,500 casualties before reaching Hungnam to be evacuated.

A COMMUNIST GENERAL is given a hearing by weary American negotiators in the Peace Pagoda at Panmunjom. Both sides agreed not to start any major offensive during the truce talks.

Deadlock on the front and at the conference table

THE Chinese armies, swollen to a half-million men, renewed their onslaught on January 1, 1951, and cleared the U.N. troops out of North Korea. By January 25 the battle line spanned the peninsula well south of Seoul. But on that day the U.N. forces launched a counteroffensive, and in April they drove most of the Chinese back into North Korea. On June 23, with the front more

or less stabilized just north of the 38th Parallel, the Russian delegate to the United Nations proposed cease-fire talks between the warring parties.

The armistice conference convened for the first time at Kaesong on July 10. Here, and later at Panmunjom, the talks ran from propaganda speeches to bitter wrangling and brief breakdowns. The war of words would last two years; meanwhile the shooting war seesawed in minor but unremitting action. Russian-built jet fighter planes made raids, then fled to safety in their Manchurian sanctuary beyond the Yalu River. Thousands of Marines and GIs died fighting savagely for shell-torn hills named Bloody, Pork Chop, Arrowhead and Heartbreak.

AN AIRLIFT by helicopter lands a Marine unit on Heartbreak Ridge six men at a time. In mountainous Korea, this novel ferrying service saved vital hours of arduous travel by truck.

A NIGHT FIGHT flares up as Marines meet an assault by waves of screaming Chinese. Amid streaking tracer bullets appear the large explosions of heavy mortar shells.

VISITING THE FRONT, President-elect Eisenhower joins GIs at lunch in December 1952. In his campaign he promised, "I shall go to Korea," but stressed that he had no "trick solution."

In truce without victory,
a legacy of bitterness

IN the spring of 1953, truce negotiators at Panmunjom agreed on a system for exchanging prisoners of war. With this main issue settled, the armistice was signed on July 27, and the guns finally fell silent along the front.

Some 3,700 American prisoners of war returned, many of them wounded or suffering from shock. They shuffled into reception centers to tell gruesome prison stories of executions, brutality and the destructive psychological techniques of "brainwashing." More than a few cried as the truth dawned on them that they were actually free. And the U.S. command realized with horror that more than 6,000 Americans had perished as captives.

In the first year of fighting a GI said, "It's the war we can't win, we can't lose, we can't quit." His bitterness was shared by most Americans in the grim aftermath of this "limited," victoryless conflict. Yet the United Nations had achieved all its objectives in Korea, and to many this gave renewed hope that Communist aggression could be contained without an atomic holocaust.

A BEWILDERED SOLDIER weeps with joy after being set free in a prisoner exchange at Panmunjom. "It's too good to be true," he kept repeating. "You're all so good to me."

4. "I LIKE IKE"

IN 1932 Franklin Roosevelt had forged a new Democratic party coalition which over the next two decades triumphed in five successive elections. So long as the memories of the Great Depression were still poignant, so long as the country was preoccupied mainly with economic issues, it seemed clear that the Democrats would prevail. But by the 1950s new issues had arisen which overshadowed the economic questions of the Roosevelt Revolution.

These issues centered on the nation's security, and most of them came to a head in a single event: the Korean War. As the party in power during three wars in 35 years, the Democrats were vulnerable to the charge that they were the "war" party. Although the decision to send American troops to Korea had received popular support, within a relatively short time this was the most unpopular war the United States had ever fought. If it should develop that it could not be fought through to total victory, the 20-year reign of the Democrats would be in jeopardy.

In late November 1950 Americans in Korea were optimistic about an early triumph. No Chinese had been seen for nearly three weeks. American commanders were convinced that there were only a few "volunteers" in Korea trying to bluff U.N. forces away from the Yalu River line. Actually, Mao's men, moving by night, were streaming across the Yalu. By mid-November 180,000 Chinese lay in the path of the Eighth Army, while 120,000 more were hidden in the mountains surrounding the Changjin Reservoir on the flank of the X Corps.

A FOREST OF PLACARDS jams the 1952 Republican convention. Demonstrations for Taft and Eisenhower were long and raucous; Stassen supporters quietly handed out roses.

Chairman of the Joint Chiefs of Staff Omar Bradley was a whipping boy for America's shocking unpreparedness in the Korean War. But Bradley was quickly exonerated: The $18 billion budget request for arms had been cut to $14.3 billion by economy-minded officials. Most importantly, ground troops had been neglected in favor of the nation's nuclear strike forces.

On November 24 MacArthur launched an "end the war" offensive. He promised his troops that they would be home for Christmas dinner. The next night the Chinese Communists struck in force. In a few days the outnumbered U.N. forces were reeling back. In sub-zero cold, through the icy month of December, they retreated steadily. The Marine survivors of the battle at the Changjin Reservoir beat a painful retreat in weather so bad that it took as many American fighting men as did the enemy. Ultimately the men of the X Corps made their way to the sea, where they were evacuated. The Chinese pushed the U.N. forces out of all the territory they had won in North Korea, again penetrated south of the 38th Parallel and recaptured Seoul.

MACARTHUR, who in September had been the hero of the Inchon maneuver, found himself in December the object of sharp criticism in the American press. He was censured for minimizing the strength of the Chinese and for deploying his troops so ineptly that they could be overwhelmed by lightly equipped Chinese infantry. Under assault, MacArthur issued public and private statements which hinted that blame for the discouraging situation in Korea lay on Washington.

As early as August 1950, the general had sent a message to the Veterans of Foreign Wars which by implication characterized the President's policy in the Far East as one of "timidity or vacillation." MacArthur believed the purpose of the war was not merely to repel the North Koreans but to eradicate Communist influence in the entire Korean peninsula. He pressed for authorization to pursue enemy planes over the Chinese border, to employ Nationalist troops from Chiang Kai-shek in the fighting, and to blockade and bomb Communist China's "privileged sanctuary" beyond the Yalu.

Many Americans shared MacArthur's impatience. In December 1950 a Montana draft board refused to induct men until MacArthur had been given a free hand to use the atomic bomb in China, although another Hiroshima might have damaged America's reputation in Asia beyond repair. House Republican leader Joseph Martin protested: "If we are not in Korea to win, then this Administration should be indicted for the murder of thousands of American boys."

But the Truman Administration, chastened by its unhappy experience with a liberation policy, now embraced the old policy of containment more fervently than ever. It refused to permit actions which might lead to all-out war with Red China. Though the Joint Chiefs of Staff briefly entertained the thought of supporting MacArthur, they changed their minds when two of their members, investigating the Korean crisis personally, found the situation not nearly so desperate as MacArthur had represented it to be. The Eighth Army was holding its own under its new leader, Lieutenant General Matthew B. Ridgway, and plans were under way for a limited counterattack.

In late January Ridgway ordered the U.N. forces to move north. By March U.N. troops recaptured Seoul and once again crossed the 38th Parallel. With South Korea liberated, Truman and the U.N. representatives believed the time was ripe for negotiation. MacArthur was informed of these plans, yet on March 24 he issued a statement, clearly in conflict with American and U.N. diplomatic efforts, which threatened Red China with the possibility of an attack on its "coastal areas and interior bases." Truman later asserted that MacArthur's statement killed any hope for an early truce.

MacArthur had been repeatedly cautioned not to make statements which conflicted with U.N. policy. His last manifesto had reached a point of disobedience which no longer could be indulged. "By this act," Truman afterward reflected, "MacArthur left me no choice—I could no longer tolerate his insubordination." Still Truman did not act. But five days before his March 24 statement MacArthur had sealed his fate. He had written Republican leader Martin: "There is no substitute for victory." He claimed "that here we fight Europe's war with arms while the diplomats there still fight it with words." On April 5 Martin read this letter on the floor of the House.

Six days later Truman dismissed MacArthur on the ground that the general was "unable to give his wholehearted support to the policies of the United States Government." Stunned by the news, the country rallied to MacArthur. Telegrams and letters to the White House ran 20-1 against the President. Flags flew at half-mast. When Truman appeared at Griffith Stadium for the opening of the baseball season, he was booed by the crowd. A Gallup poll revealed that only 29 per cent of Americans interviewed supported him. G.O.P. leaders agreed that the general should be invited to address Congress and that there should be a probe of the Administration's policy. "In addition," Martin told newsmen bluntly, "the question of impeachments was discussed."

In a dramatic address to a joint meeting of Congress on April 19, 1951, MacArthur defended his opposition to limited war: "Why, my soldiers asked of me, surrender military advantages to an enemy in the field?" After a dramatic pause he went on: "I could not answer." He concluded his talk with a reference to a barracks-room ballad of his youth "which proclaimed most proudly that 'old soldiers never die; they just fade away.' And like the old soldier of that ballad, I now close my military career and just fade away, an old soldier who tried to do his duty as God gave him the light to see that duty. Good-by."

In his 34-minute address MacArthur was interrupted by fervent applause 30 times. Congressman Dewey Short of Missouri (who had been educated at Harvard, Oxford and Heidelberg) cried out that he had seen "God in the flesh, the voice of God." Herbert Hoover saw the general as "a reincarnation of St. Paul into a great General of the Army who came out of the East."

But the MacArthur frenzy failed to survive a congressional investigation that spring. From May 3 to June 25 the country learned that, contrary to MacArthur's claim, the Joint Chiefs of Staff supported the President against the general. Critics of MacArthur protested that his attack on the concept of limited war rested on the assumption that small losses in limited conflicts were unjustifiable while colossal losses in all-out war were acceptable. MacArthur's approach, General Omar Bradley, Chairman of the Joint Chiefs of Staff, observed, "would involve us in the wrong war, at the wrong place, at the wrong time, and with the wrong enemy."

BUT the ending of the MacArthur episode did not stop the controversy over the Korean War and America's foreign policy. A week after the general's dismissal, Senator Vandenberg died. With his moderating influence gone, the conservatives led by Senator Taft made a bold bid to win control of the Republican party and, in the 1952 elections, of the government. Before long Taft, who had once supported American participation in the Korea conflict, was calling it an "unnecessary war," and "a Truman war."

In his campaign for the Republican presidential nomination Taft was supported by a majority of the G.O.P. delegation in Congress. But internationalist

THE KOREAN WAR:

CHANGJIN TO PANMUNJOM

The war was five months old when United Nations forces, renewing the offensive along the battle line (1), were sent reeling backward by Chinese Communist attacks. One group, cut off at Changjin Reservoir, had to fight through to Hungnam (2) to be evacuated. In retreat, the U.N. forces again gave up Seoul (3) before they formed an effective defense line (4). Then a new U.N. offensive retook Seoul (5). For two years, during truce talks at Panmunjom, the fighting seesawed along the 38th Parallel. A dotted line (6) marks the front at the signing of the armistice.

This photograph of Adlai Stevenson's campaign-worn shoe (above) provided a light moment in the hard-fought 1952 presidential campaign. Later, when a riot erupted in an Illinois prison, Governor Stevenson sped home and halted it (below). Republican Richard M. Nixon was quick to assert that Stevenson was more interested in a local riot than in the Korean war.

party members disapproved of Taft's record of isolationism and doubted that he could win. They hoped to draft a man who was a national hero and who had never sought political office: General of the Army Dwight D. Eisenhower, then serving as Supreme Commander of NATO forces in Europe, having taken a leave of absence from his duties as president of Columbia University. There was, however, doubt that "Ike," as he was affectionately known, would be willing to run—and even some question that he was a Republican.

On January 6, 1952, after flying to Paris to confer with the general, Senator Henry Cabot Lodge told a crowded press conference in Washington that Eisenhower was in the race "to the finish." In France the NATO commander confirmed that he was a Republican and that he would not interfere with Lodge's move to enter him in the New Hampshire primary that spring. Despite Ike's absence in Europe while Taft stumped New Hampshire, the general defeated the senator in the primary by 10,000 votes.

Yet Taft showed strength too. He edged out Eisenhower at the North Carolina state convention and on one day won primaries in Wisconsin and Nebraska. If the general were to wage an effective campaign, he would have to return to America. Accordingly Eisenhower asked to be relieved as NATO commander.

EISENHOWER'S first campaign speech—at his home town of Abilene, Kansas, on June 4—proved disappointing. It was clear that he needed an issue to bolster his claim that he was the candidate of "the people" running against the organization politician, Taft. He found one in the swiftly developing battle for control of the 38 convention votes of Texas.

Some weeks earlier Eisenhower's supporters in Texas, finding the Taft forces in control of the Republican state convention, had organized a rump convention and elected a rival slate of delegates. The general's backers claimed the Taft people were trying to steal the delegation; Ike denounced the Taft backers as "rustlers" who had purloined "the Texas birthright." The case against Taft was a weak one; many of Eisenhower's supporters in Texas were Democrats who had voted in the Republican primaries, and Taft's organization denounced this invasion. But by convention time Eisenhower's backers had created the image of the general as the spokesman for clean government, while portraying Taft as a sordid manipulator.

When the credentials committee held its sessions in Chicago under the naked lights of the TV cameras, Taft's delegates appeared to bad advantage. Amid great uproar, the Eisenhower delegates were seated. When the voting on candidates began, the general won the nomination on the first ballot. For its vice presidential nominee, the convention chose 39-year-old Senator Richard M. Nixon of California, a decision which recognized both the importance of the Pacific Coast and the vote-getting potential of the Communist issue.

Eisenhower's enormous popularity would have made him a hard man to beat under the best of circumstances, and his chances were heightened by evidences of corruption in the Truman Administration. Assistant Attorney General T. Lamar Caudle was implicated in the acceptance of costly gifts from "fixers" and from persons accused of tax frauds. A Senate investigation had turned up a group of "five percenters," who peddled their influence in government for a commission. Very damaging was testimony that a company which wanted help in Washington had given the President's military aide, Harry Vaughan, a freezer and through Vaughan distributed other units to officials. Even more notoriety resulted from an investigation of the Reconstruction Finance Corporation by Senator Fulbright. Among other things, it was disclosed that the wife of a former RFC loan examiner had been aided in acquiring a $9,540 mink coat by an attorney for a firm which had applied for an RFC loan. Together with "deep-freeze" and "five percenter," "mink coat" became a symbol for immorality in the federal government.

With the Truman Administration tarred by the responsibility for scandal in Washington, the country looked for a new political figure to lead it once more onto the paths of righteousness. Some Democrats thought they might have such a leader in the lanky senator from Tennessee, Estes Kefauver. While the RFC probe was at its height, Kefauver was winning national attention by summoning gangsters before his special crime investigation committee. Little was actually achieved by the hearings, but the senator whipped up the country's indignation at the effrontery of gang leaders and the venality of local governments. Thousands stayed away from work to gaze at the televised hearings. Women ignored their children and their housework. In Philadelphia a man intently watched the hearings while fire swept his house.

In 1952 Kefauver, now a national figure, made a strong bid for the Democratic presidential nomination. A coonskin cap on his head, he turned up on street corners to shake hands with voters. He made a good showing in primaries, but he never had a chance. His liberal record had alienated fellow Southerners, and many liberals thought him an intellectual lightweight. More important, Democratic chieftains held him responsible for the defeat of party candidates in cities where graft was an issue, and he had antagonized party leaders by announcing his candidacy before Truman had bowed out of the race.

Truman himself set out to win the nomination for a man little known to the American people: Adlai E. Stevenson. A graduate of Princeton whose grandfather had been Vice President in Cleveland's second term, Stevenson was the articulate and witty governor of Illinois, and he had a varied career of government service behind him. But with typical reticence and self-doubt, Stevenson refused to run. By the eve of the Chicago convention a draft-Stevenson movement had built up tremendous momentum. As Democratic governor of the host state, Stevenson welcomed the delegates with an eloquent speech that ruined whatever hope he might still have held of avoiding the nomination. He was nominated on the third ballot.

I N his acceptance speech, Stevenson set the tone of his campaign: "The ordeal of the Twentieth Century—the bloodiest, most turbulent era of the Christian age—is far from over. Sacrifice, patience, understanding and implacable purpose may be our lot for years to come. Let's face it. Let's talk sense to the American people. Let's tell them the truth, that there are no gains without pains, that we are now on the eve of great decisions. . . ."

In the remarkable campaign that followed, Stevenson told voters some hard truths. He warned the American Legion that a veteran was someone who owed America more than the nation owed him. He told a Labor Day rally in Detroit that he did not think the Taft-Hartley Act was a slave-labor law. In Richmond, Virginia, the governor announced his support of a program of civil rights for Negroes. Stevenson captivated intellectuals with his incisive wit, his eloquence, and his troubled recognition of the problems the world faced and the need for intelligence and fortitude to meet them. But everyone knew

In the tradition of Davy Crockett, Estes Kefauver wore a coonskin cap as his trademark in his bid for the 1952 Democratic presidential nomination. Kefauver was strong in his native Tennessee, but he had almost no national organization. He did most of his campaigning on his own, inspiring Daniel Fitzpatrick to caption the above cartoon "The Lone Ranger."

that support by the intellectuals—or, in a word born during the campaign, the "eggheads"—did not add up to many votes on Election Day.

At the outset, the inexperienced Eisenhower proved a poor campaigner, but gradually he began to find himself. He was assisted by a large-scale advertising campaign, and major cities were inundated with spot television commercials aimed at "selling" the candidate to the voters. But Eisenhower needed no selling. The popular response to the general was tremendous and spontaneous. People who shouted "I like Ike" meant it. Americans warmed to his radiant grin, were cheered by his salute with both hands raised above his head, and were heartened by the man's fundamental decency and humility.

Satirizing Eisenhower's ineffectual resistance to McCarthyism, this Herblock cartoon has Ike brandishing a feather as a warning to the senator to "Have a care, sir." While the President often defended his Administration against Joe McCarthy's attacks, Eisenhower never replied in kind because, as he privately said, "I will not get in the gutter with that guy."

THE only serious problem the general faced was the division in the party caused by the failure of Taft to win the nomination. Taft himself gave Eisenhower a formal endorsement, but left the impression that he might choose to sit out the campaign. To win Taft to his cause, Eisenhower invited the Ohioan to the house in New York's Morningside Heights that he had occupied as president of Columbia University. Taft emerged with the announcement that he had won Ike's acceptance of a manifesto he had drafted which embodied the conservative viewpoint on domestic affairs. Eisenhower, the senator declared, was in accord with Taft's view that the main threat to the country's liberty came from the "constant growth of big government" and that the main issue of the campaign was liberty against "creeping socialization." Taft conceded that he and Eisenhower were not wholly in accord on foreign policy, but the senator thought the differences were only "differences of degree." The Morningside Heights conference healed the rupture in the party. Taft began to campaign actively. Democratic critics charged that Eisenhower had "surrendered," but the pact suggested less that the candidate had capitulated to Taft than that his views were unexpectedly close to Taft's.

Eisenhower's critics also took issue with his attitude toward McCarthyism. McCarthy and his followers posed a special problem for Eisenhower: They were party colleagues, but they had engaged in vicious criticism of Ike's old chief and patron, General Marshall. McCarthy had accused Marshall of being part of "a conspiracy so immense, an infamy so black, as to dwarf any previous such venture in the history of man." Nonetheless Eisenhower permitted McCarthy to ride on his campaign train in Wisconsin, and when the general spoke in Milwaukee, he deleted a paragraph praising Marshall. Eisenhower also repeated the charge that the Democrats were soft on Communism. ("We have seen this sort of thing go on and on until my running mate, Dick Nixon, grabbed a police whistle and stopped it.") Nixon, for his part, called Stevenson "Adlai the appeaser . . . who got a Ph.D. from Dean Acheson's College of Cowardly Communist Containment."

Young, vigorous, a hard fighter, Nixon delighted the Republican regulars. But on September 18 the New York Post revealed that Nixon, as senator, had been subsidized by California millionaires through a secret fund which, it subsequently developed, totaled $18,000 in a year and a half. Nixon's conservative voting record left him open to the charge that by his votes on taxation and housing he was repaying the men who had financed him.

For a party crusading against Democratic immorality, nothing could have been more embarrassing. Eisenhower insisted that if Nixon was to stay on the ticket he would have to demonstrate that he was "as clean as a hound's tooth." But before deciding whether to ditch Nixon, Ike agreed to wait until the senator had made a public defense on radio and TV.

An estimated 55 million Americans turned their dials to Nixon that night as he told the Horatio Alger story of his life: his rise from poor circumstances (as a boy he had worked in a grocery store); his war record in the South Pacific ("I guess I'm entitled to a couple of stars . . . but I was just there when the bombs were falling"); and his wife Pat who did not have a mink coat but did have "a respectable Republican cloth coat." Nixon related that a supporter had sent his little girls a dog that his daughter had named Checkers. "And you know the kids, like all kids, love the dog, and I just want to say this right now, that regardless of what they say about it, we're going to keep it."

Nixon's critics called it a slick soap-opera performance, but the Republicans were deluged with messages approving Nixon. When Nixon flew to Wheeling, West Virginia, Eisenhower, with tears in his eyes, extended his hand and said: "Dick, you're my boy." With the ticket reunited and Nixon far more popular than he had been, the Republicans were stronger than ever.

The formula for the Republican campaign was, in Senator Karl Mundt's words, K_1C_2—Korea, corruption and Communism. Of this trinity of issues, Korea was much the most potent. After U.N. forces turned back three Chinese offensives in the spring of 1951 with heavy losses, the Communists had agreed to armistice negotiations. Month after month, the truce parley dragged on. Meanwhile, to bring pressure on the negotiators, the Americans launched periodic limited offensives. In the summer and fall of 1951, thousands died to take insignificant knobs on Bloody Ridge or Heartbreak Ridge. Although there were no large engagements, casualties continued to mount, and it seemed as though this war might go on forever, hopelessly, pointlessly.

One consequence of the Korean War appeared, on the surface, to benefit Democrats. The war detonated a skyrocketing economic boom in the United States which brought the country unparalleled prosperity. But even this was turned against the Democrats, for the war boom was steeped in guilt. Prosperity seemed to have been paid for in blood. Moreover, along with the boom came higher prices—and, inevitably, the hated controls.

O N October 24 in Detroit, Eisenhower delivered the master stroke of the campaign. The general pledged to bring the war in Korea to "an early and honorable end." To achieve this, he promised, "I shall go to Korea."

On Election Day, Eisenhower won a landslide victory: 442 electoral votes to Stevenson's 89. Eisenhower was the first Republican candidate since 1928 to break the Democratic hold on the "Solid South," taking Virginia, Tennessee, Florida and Texas. But the triumph was a personal one for Ike rather than for his party. The G.O.P. had a House majority of only eight and an even split in the Senate; Vice President Nixon's vote, however, gave them a margin of one in case of a tie.

For Eisenhower the greatest challenges still lay ahead. He faced fearful tasks: to terminate the fighting in Korea without loss of honor or prestige; to accommodate to the revolution of rising expectations in the colonial world; to curb McCarthy, now nearing the apex of his power, and bring the era of bad feeling to a close. To these tasks, Eisenhower brought the advantage of enormous prestige. As 20 years of Democratic rule came to an end, the most crucial issue of all was what the new President would do with his great power.

Some political sages had predicted a long struggle for the 1952 Republican presidential nomination. But the delegates selected General Eisenhower on the first ballot, leaving "Mr. Republican," Robert Taft, as a political wallflower for the third time. It proved a wise choice; no matter what language it was said in, the voters—55.14 per cent of them—really liked Ike.

A SADDENED GROUP, shaken by F.D.R.'s death only hours earlier, watches as Harry Truman is sworn in as President by Chief Justice Harlan Stone on April 12, 1945. Three women were present—Mrs. Truman *(center)*, daughter Margaret *(left of Stone)* and Labor Secretary Frances Perkins. Other members of Roosevelt's Cabinet, congressmen and officials looked on.

Awesome tasks for Harry and Ike

HARRY S. TRUMAN'S hometown of Independence, Missouri, and Dwight Eisenhower's Abilene, Kansas, lie less than 150 miles apart. Both men came of hard-working, religious families of modest means; both had a style which seemed typically American—simple and open in manner, colloquial in speech. Both were more at home with rank-and-file voters than with intellectuals. Both distrusted rigid ideologies, and both served in the first peacetime period when an American President could not concentrate on domestic affairs and ignore world problems.

Yet nothing could have been more different than the circumstances under which each took office. Truman, the relatively obscure Vice President, a former senator who prided himself on being a politician, later recalled that his oath-taking *(above)* "lasted hardly more than a minute." General of the Army Eisenhower, the illustrious commander who considered himself above politics, came in to boisterous cheers as a self-described "crusader" determined to start a "spiritual" awakening in American political life. More than 100,000 persons happily watched Eisenhower's inauguration *(opposite)*. Truman's first days in office were shadowed by the powerful personality of his predecessor, whose presence millions had felt was indispensable to the winning of the war and the peace to come. Eisenhower, a world figure in his own right, entered with the adulation of the G.O.P., for which he had ended a 20-year drought, and the affection of a nation which saw in his friendliness the promise of peace.

A SPLENDID CEREMONY, Eisenhower's first inauguration, on January 20, 1953, sees Truman, Eisenhower and Nixon listening to the Marine Band from the East Capitol steps.

MAKING A NAME with his Truman Committee from 1941 to 1944, the Missouri senator probes inefficiency in the national defense program as head of the special investigating body.

The "Year of Decisions" for the man from Missouri

FEW American Presidents have taken office during a more demanding period, or with less adequate preparation, than Harry Truman. Never a member of F.D.R.'s inner circle, Truman recalled that during his 82 days as Vice President, he had had few opportunities to confer with the President. Now, though poorly briefed, Truman had to make his own decisions at a time when world events were moving at a breakneck pace. The San Francisco Conference, setting up the United Nations, was to start two weeks after he took office. In three months the "Big Three" would hold the Potsdam Conference near Berlin *(right);* there Truman was to meet the leaders of England and Russia to discuss plans for revitalizing war-torn Europe and achieving quick victory over Japan. The Yalta agreements with Russia were already dissolving in mistrust. In the European theater victory seemed at hand, but victory would bring further problems—the economy of Europe was devastated, and Stalin was beginning to establish Communist regimes in the territories on Russia's western frontiers. The Japanese were on the run, but the reopening of hostilities between the Chinese Nationalists and Reds meant that peace in the Far East was remote. Truman, whose prime accomplishment to date had been as chairman of a widely respected Senate investigating committee *(above),* suddenly had the world's burdens on his shoulders. When he later wrote his memoirs, he devoted half the space to the first of his nearly eight years in office and entitled this volume "Year of Decisions."

PONDERING THE SHAPE of the postwar world, the new President is seen at the end of the Potsdam Conference in August 1945 with British Prime Minister Attlee *(left),* Joseph Stalin.

A FEARFUL CHOICE, Truman's order to drop the A-bomb
(right) on Japan in August 1945 is still hotly debated.
But Truman "never lost any sleep over" his decision.

A surprise victory for an underrated candidate

ONE of the white doves released to welcome Truman to the Democratic convention in June 1948 soared high, smashed into the balcony of Philadelphia's Convention Hall and dropped to the floor. "A dead pigeon," said a lackadaisical delegate, looking at the President. Since the first of the year, Truman's popularity had fallen precipitously. For three years Truman had turned most of his energy to foreign policy; his critics were assailing his "neglect" of domestic affairs. But shouting, "I will win this election," he now embarked on one of the most vigorous political campaigns in U.S. history.

He purposefully recalled the Republican Congress, knowing it would not act on his welfare proposals in the short session. Then he boarded a train for a long series of whistle-stop talks in which he heaped scorn on the "do-nothing" Congress. By the end of his tour, Truman was outdrawing G.O.P. candidate Thomas E. Dewey. Even so, his narrow victory, despite the defections of the Dixiecrats and Progressives, was so unexpected that many papers prematurely announced Truman's defeat.

Speaking "plainly and bluntly" in Oklahoma, Truman presses his 1948 campaign. He often introduced his wife and daughter with homey

CHURCHILL'S WARNING against Soviet expansion is pondered by Truman (*left*) at Fulton, Missouri, in 1946. Truman's moves to stem the Russians heightened his differences with Commerce Secretary Henry Wallace; later Truman fired him.

humor as "the boss" and "the boss's boss."

Truman's "just folks" appeal enlivens a press conference during his 1951 vacation at Key West.

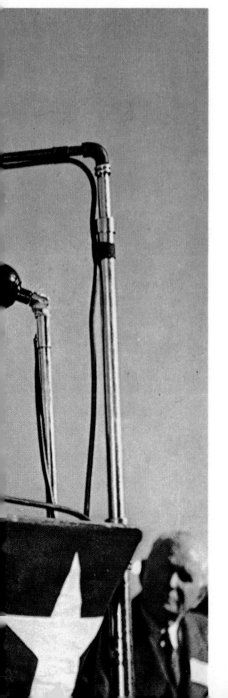

An Allied plane brings food and fuel to civilians blockaded in Berlin by the Russians. On one day of the 11-month airlift, almost 13,000 tons

SECURING THE WEST with a 12-nation defense pact, Secretary of State Dean Acheson signs the North Atlantic Treaty on April 4, 1949. Truman and Vice President Barkley look on.

Bold actions to stem the Soviet tide

THE turning point in America's foreign policy," said Truman, came in 1947. He extended aid to the Communist-threatened governments of Greece and Turkey and followed up with Marshall Plan aid to all of non-Communist Europe. As Truman put it, "Russia was caught off guard by the Marshall Plan" and decided to "test our firmness" by cutting off access to Berlin from the West. On June 26, 1948, Truman ordered all U.S. planes in Europe to fly supplies *(above)* to the West Berliners. The incredible success of this operation brought Soviet capitulation after nearly a year. In 1949 America's course was clearly marked by a commitment to fight if necessary to protect Western Europe under the North Atlantic Treaty, called by Truman "a shield against aggression." A similar pact earlier in the century, he declared, would have prevented the two world wars.

In the Far East the Cold War became a shooting war as South Korea was invaded in June 1950 by Soviet-backed North Koreans, later reinforced by Red Chinese troops. Although the Korean conflict was still raging in 1951, Truman was by then confident that his actions had forestalled a third World War. Many observers felt that in his years in the White House, Truman had made so many important decisions and surmounted so many crises that his place in history was solidly entrenched.

of supplies were flown in. Truman said the airlift showed Europe "that we would act, and act resolutely, when . . . freedom was threatened."

SECURING THE EAST through force of arms raises issues that bring Truman to Wake Island in October 1950 to confer with General MacArthur on Korean policy. In a surprise cere-mony *(above)* Truman awarded MacArthur a Distinguished Service Medal. But six months later, when Truman felt the gen-eral's statements had become insubordinate, he sacked him.

HONORED WAR HERO Eisenhower and his wife Mamie, at the White House, listen as Truman—six weeks after V-E Day—reads the citation for Ike's third Distinguished Service Medal.

A friendship sundered in the switch to the G.O.P.

THEIR association had been close enough so that Eisenhower presented Truman with the globe he had used in the war, and Truman was widely rumored to favor Ike as his successor if the general would run as a Democrat. But by the time the Republican party took power, they were barely on speaking terms. In 1959 Eisenhower, prompted by his guest Winston Churchill, invited Truman to the White House; Truman declined. Their antagonism began in the 1952 campaign: Ike was promising "to clean up the mess in Washington," and Truman was speaking on behalf of Adlai Stevenson. Eisenhower was informed that Truman had quipped, "Ike has a brass halo." When Ike blamed Truman for blunders that led to the Korean War and vowed "to go to Korea in person if elected and put an end to the fighting," Truman labeled the trip "a piece of demagoguery." After their meetings to arrange the transfer of power, Truman told his aides, "Poor Ike—it won't be a bit like the Army. He'll find it very frustrating." On inauguration day they rode through Washington in silence until Ike angrily asked who was responsible for flying his son from duty in Korea to Washington—an act embarrassing to Eisenhower. Truman answered: "The President of the United States ordered your son to attend your inauguration."

ALIENATED PRESIDENTS Eisenhower and Truman make conversation on Ike's inauguration day. On the day of John F. Kennedy's funeral in 1963 they resumed cordial relations.

JUBILANT REPUBLICANS celebrate Ike's first inauguration at a ball in the Washington Armory. A guest needed an hour to fight his way in and 20 minutes to get out.

ENJOYING HIS ROLE as a politician, President Eisenhower arrives in San Francisco for the 1956 Republican Convention a day earlier than expected. He explained that "A few days ago I was reading the papers and I suddenly decided this was too interesting a place to stay away from . . ." He was renominated by acclamation, with Richard Nixon again his running mate.

94

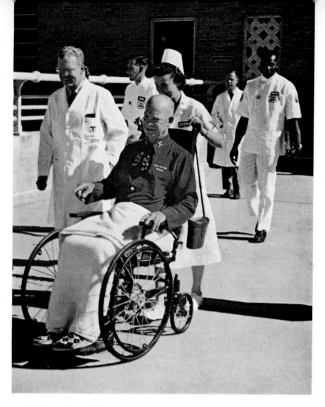

ON THE LINKS in Georgia with G.O.P. Senator Robert Taft, Ike follows his shot. Before Taft drove, Ike said: "We'll put some pressure on the legislative branch now. Come on, Bob."

RECOVERING from his 1955 heart attack, Ike sports five gold Army stars and a silver one awarded by his doctor for "good conduct." His pajamas also bear a note, "Much better thanks."

Personal victory over illness and frustration

To Eisenhower, the change of roles from military commander to the highest civilian job in the land often brought a combination of personal triumph and political stalemate. Early in his Administration he was astonished by the maneuvering of G.O.P. leaders for partisan purposes. To Senate Leader William Knowland, who had opposed most of his plans for defense and foreign aid, Ike snapped: "My God, you just can't sit back and assume the nation is safe from all harm because the Republicans won the last election." But if he was not always able to keep his party in his own image, he enjoyed such huge popularity that he could shrug off criticism of his penchant for golf. Surmounting the personal trials of three serious illnesses, Ike stuck to his own style of leadership, which he described as "persuasion—and conciliation—and education—and patience."

Ike concentrates as he talks strategy in February 1954 with G.O.P. leaders (left to right) Smith, Millikin, Ferguson, Knowland and Martin.

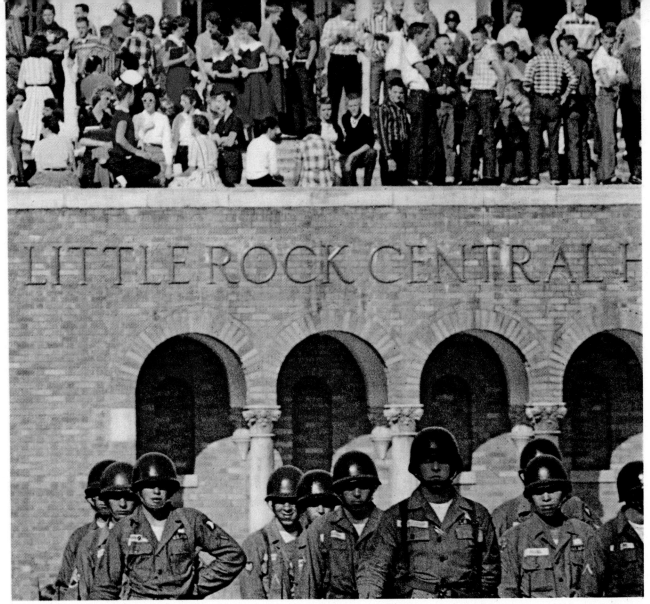

Armed and alert, paratroopers sent by presidential order enforce integration at Little Rock's Central High School on September 25, 1957.

The critical tests of Ike's second term

IN the final days of the 1956 presidential campaign, war erupted in the Middle East with an Anglo-French-Israeli assault on Egypt. Russia threatened to come to Egypt's aid. Eisenhower put America's weight behind pressures in the United Nations which ended hostilities in a little more than a week and brought a settlement the following year.

Eisenhower's ability was repeatedly tested during his second term by other crises. In September 1957 he federalized the Arkansas National Guard and sent regulars to Little Rock to enforce a court order requiring school integration—even though, as Sherman Adams declared, the move was "a constitutional duty which was the most repugnant to him of all his acts in his eight years at the White House." The critics—who said an earlier firm

stand would have obviated any possibility of trouble with Arkansas Governor Faubus—roared again a month later when Russia sent *Sputnik I*, the first man-made satellite, into successful orbit. In the spring of 1960 when a U-2 reconnaissance plane was shot down on Russian territory, the Administration fumbled—first denying, then accepting responsibility for aerial espionage. Eisenhower brushed off detractors. The satellite launching, he said, "does not raise my apprehensions, not one iota." As for the Russians' attitude about the U-2: "It's absolutely ridiculous," he protested, "and they know it." In 1958 Americans, shaken by Russian space exploits, could take some comfort from their own satellites, and in 1959 could point with pride to a new achievement in space communications *(opposite, above).*

A U-2 SPY PLANE is identical to the one downed by Soviet rockets in May 1960. Angered by the incident, Premier Khrushchev canceled Eisenhower's scheduled visit to the Soviet Union.

OUTER-SPACE RELAY enables Eisenhower to hear his voice from a satellite. This rebroadcast of Ike's 1958 Christmas message was an achievement, but short of Russian space triumphs.

MIDDLE EAST CRISIS is evidenced by one of 14 ships sunk to block the Suez Canal during the Anglo-French-Israeli attack that followed Egyptian plans to nationalize the vital canal.

Personal diplomacy and a pilgrimage of peace

I SET forth as your agent," said the man on television, "to extend once again to millions of people across the seas assurance of America's sincere friendship. I know you wish me well." Thus Eisenhower spoke to Americans on December 3, 1959, on the eve of an 11-nation tour of Asia, Africa and Europe, part of the most far-ranging diplomatic effort of any American chief executive. He rode through streets jammed with cheering throngs, met such diverse leaders as Pope John XXIII and Mohammed Ayub Khan, president of Pakistan.

In his last two years in office, Eisenhower took hold of American foreign policy in a manner so dramatic as to confound the pundits who had expected him to act like a "lame duck" President. In the summer of 1959, he flew to Great Britain, France and West Germany. That autumn he entertained Khrushchev on a state visit which produced hopes—later dashed by the U-2 incident—of a new East-West *détente*. In 1960 he went to South America and to the Far East. At every stop he drew record crowds. With few exceptions, his welcome seemed proof that the Eisenhower magnetism was truly international. Commented the New York *Times:* "Hereafter Uncle Sam will look like President Eisenhower—a man who did not pretend good will but honestly felt it."

Standing at attention behind their flags, Eisenhower and Khrushchev listen to their national anthems on the Soviet premier's arrival on

IN KARACHI Ike rides with Pakistani President Ayub Khan, who told him that the big crowds shouting *"Zindabad!"* were wishing him a long life.

IN THE VATICAN LIBRARY President Eisenhower and Pope John XXIII are joined by Ike's son John and daughter-in-law Barbara. The pontiff surprised his American visitors by delivering a short speech in English.

September 15, 1959, at Andrews Air Force Base. In the background is the giant Soviet TU-114 that flew Khrushchev to the portentous meeting.

5. THE MIDDLE OF THE ROAD

THE 33,936,000 Americans who voted Dwight D. Eisenhower into the presidency in 1952 did so for a variety of reasons. Some believed that he, as a nonpolitical figure of great stature, could restore national unity. Some anticipated that he would use his immense prestige to move the nation in new directions. Many Republicans who had never been reconciled to the changes wrought by Roosevelt and Truman hoped that he would do away with these innovations. But some seem to have backed him primarily because they hoped he would liberate them from the oppressive burdens of politics.

The country was to discover that it was not easy to turn away from public affairs. The United States was a mighty power in a world threatened by Communist tyranny and the disaster of thermonuclear war. To achieve national unity, it might for the moment postpone facing up to critical problems, but the problems would not go away.

The path to America's future, Eisenhower once stated, was "down the middle." To achieve the middle way, Ike sought to achieve a "revolution" in the national government, "trying to make it smaller rather than bigger and finding things it can stop doing instead of seeking new things for it to do." Eisenhower, more conservative than most supposed, would often find the middle of the road in domestic affairs, but only after veering well to the right.

The President's Cabinet was an index to his political orientation. Eisenhower named Charles E. Wilson, president of General Motors, as Secretary of

A POPULAR LEADER, Dwight D. Eisenhower is seen amid mementos of his military career. His appeal prompted a multitude of Democrats to vote for him as President.

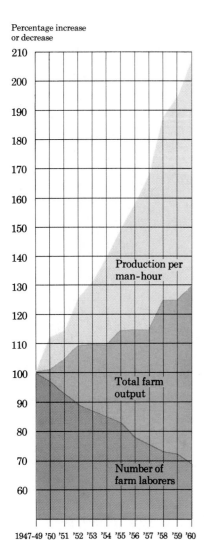

Percentage increase
or decrease

Production per
man-hour

Total farm
output

Number of
farm laborers

1947-49 '50 '51 '52 '53 '54 '55 '56 '57 '58 '59 '60

A FARM TREND: FEWER
MEN, GREATER YIELD

*America's swift advances in agri-
cultural automation and technology during the 1950s created major
political and sociological problems.
From 1949 to 1960 production rose
almost one third (center of chart)
while the number of farm workers
(bottom of chart) fell off by about
the same amount. Total productivity per man-hour (at top of chart)
more than doubled. Pushing buttons, a single farmer in 10 minutes could feed 400 cows and 500 pigs.
A few years before, it would have
taken five men half a day. The result: an emptying countryside and
a vast glut of many farm products.*

Defense; George Humphrey, president of M. A. Hanna Company, to be Secre-
tary of the Treasury; two wealthy former General Motors dealers, Douglas Mc-
Kay and Arthur Summerfield, to the posts of Secretary of the Interior and
Postmaster General; and a New England industrialist, Sinclair Weeks, as
Secretary of Commerce. Secretary of State John Foster Dulles had been a
wealthy corporation lawyer. Other appointees were generally of a conservative stamp: Secretary of Agriculture Ezra Benson; Attorney General Herbert
Brownell Jr.; and as head of the newly formed department of Health, Educa-
tion and Welfare, Mrs. Oveta Culp Hobby, wife of a wealthy Texas publisher.
The one marked exception was Secretary of Labor Martin Durkin, a Stevenson man who had been president of the international plumbers' union. The
Cabinet, suggested one writer, consisted of "eight millionaires and a
plumber." By September 1953 Durkin had resigned.

Many were dismayed that Eisenhower, who was regarded as the spokesman for the national interest, had chosen a Cabinet that appeared to rep-
resent only a single interest. Even before the Administration took office,
Wilson added fuel to the fire. In the midst of hearings on his appointment
(which aroused concern over a possible conflict of interest, since General
Motors was the largest single contractor to the Defense Department), Wilson
announced: "I thought what was good for our country was good for General
Motors, and vice versa." Circulated in a twisted form ("What is good for
General Motors is good for the country"), the remark reinforced the impression
in some quarters that big business had captured the government. The impression was not diminished when Douglas McKay remarked, "We're here in the
saddle as an administration representing business and industry."

The most influential Cabinet member was Secretary of the Treasury Humphrey, a man whom the President admired and trusted. "In Cabinet meetings,"
Eisenhower said, "I always wait for George Humphrey to speak. . . . I know
that when he speaks he will say just what I am thinking."

Humphrey and Eisenhower shared a common fear of inflation and a distaste
for deficits. Their determination to maintain a stable dollar was to set the
guidelines for the Administration's policy in both foreign and domestic affairs.
Under Humphrey's aegis the Administration immediately sought to cut back
federal spending, meanwhile raising interest rates. Government bonds
slumped, and by May *Business Week* was grumbling: "We are glad to know
the brakes work, but we don't want to go through the windshield." Within a
few weeks, Humphrey was softening his tight-money approach.

MEANWHILE, as part of the major change in government he hoped to
achieve, Eisenhower advanced the "partnership" theory for the development of the nation's resources. Instead of relying so largely on the federal
government, as Roosevelt and Truman had, he proposed to encourage development by local governments and by private interests. Federal dam projects
were shelved, regulatory agencies were staffed with men sympathetic to the
utilities, and the offshore oil lands were turned over to the adjacent states.

Six months after he took office, Eisenhower explained that he was trying
to roll back the "creeping socialism" of the past 20 years, and he cited expansion of the Tennessee Valley Authority. The attempt to circumvent TVA
led the President into the major embarrassment of his first term.

Instead of permitting TVA to build a steam plant to provide power for the

Memphis area, the Administration authorized the Atomic Energy Commission to contract with the Dixon-Yates utility combine to produce the power. Democrats protested that the deal not only amounted to a giveaway to the utilities, but that it had been negotiated under suspicious circumstances. In February 1955 a Senate committee revealed that one Adolphe Wenzell had served as a consultant to the Budget Bureau while he was financially connected with the Dixon-Yates combine. The following July the President canceled the contract. When Dixon-Yates sued to recoup its losses, the Department of Justice responded that the contract, in which the Administration had taken such pride, had been illegal and "contrary to the public interest" from the very beginning. Fought up to the Supreme Court, the case was finally decided against the utility.

Joseph W. Martin became Speaker of the House when the Republicans roared back into the congressional majority in 1946. The title of Speaker was ironic for Martin. As a boy he had stuttered so badly that he often wept with embarrassment. But he would "cry and fight like hell all at the same time."

AMONG the most intractable of all the problems that Eisenhower confronted was the farm question. Even in boom times, the farmer had been in serious trouble. Although the farm population decreased by nearly seven million in the 1950s, output grew so remarkably that production vastly outstripped demand. Each year fewer farmers raised a greater yield; each year the surpluses mounted. To bolster rural income, the Truman Administration had maintained high, rigid price supports.

Benson's program of flexible and lower price supports on certain commodities, which replaced the previous schedule of fixed supports, was a costly failure. In addition he restricted credit and curtailed the rural electrification program. Market prices continued to drop, and from 1952 to 1956 the farmer's share of the national income fell from 6.4 per cent to scarcely 4.1 per cent. In sections of the Midwest Benson's name was anathema. A Missouri tenant farmer complained: "We've been plagued by one year of flood, three years of drought and two years of Benson." The Administration was compelled to compromise on various new forms of subsidies. By 1959 the government was spending six times as much on agriculture as in 1952.

Benson's experience was typical. There was often a wide gap between the Eisenhower Administration's generally conservative doctrine and its practice. When a cut in government spending triggered a moderate recession in 1953-1954, Humphrey borrowed New Deal techniques, including a tax cut, an increase in social security payments and extension of unemployment compensation, to help bring the country through the downturn by late 1954. After Eisenhower's eight years in office, the federal government was intervening in the economy in much the same fashion as when he entered the White House. Moreover, despite his belief in fiscal responsibility, his two Administrations accumulated a deficit of $21.9 billion; the $12.4 billion deficit of 1959 set a peacetime record. The Eisenhower budgets ran higher than all but one of the Truman budgets.

When Sam Rayburn was a young boy he knew exactly what job he wanted: Speaker of the House of Representatives. Elected to Congress in 1912, he was later Speaker for an unprecedented 17 years. "Mr. Sam" spent nearly half a century in the House and said of it: "I love the House of Representatives."

Yet Eisenhower's concept of the presidency was attuned to the mood of moderation. Convinced that Roosevelt and Truman had overstepped the bounds of proper executive action with regard to Congress, Eisenhower sought to "restore" the balance between the executive and legislative branches. He limited his own role to one of suggesting policies and then leaving congressmen free to "vote their own consciences." Nor did Eisenhower believe in imposing his will on his own Administration. He organized his staff on military lines, with Sherman Adams, former governor of New Hampshire, charged

Ezra Taft Benson seemed the perfect choice for Secretary of Agriculture: He was born on a farm, studied agricultural economics and had worked as a county agricultural agent. But his steps toward a free market in agriculture enraged the farm population. In 1959 a group of Iowa farmers, with the approval of their Democratic governor, hanged Benson in effigy.

with regulating the flow of information to the President. Critics objected that this military staff arrangement limited the President to policies that had been screened and approved by his subordinates, and that he was extraordinarily isolated from information that did not flow through channels.

Eisenhower's reluctance to use his authority either with respect to Congress or in the councils of his party left him at the mercy of right-wing Republicans who seemed determined to assert their supremacy over the Executive. The President had fair success in his relations with Taft, but after the Ohioan died of cancer on July 31, 1953, G.O.P. conservatives became more rambunctious. They killed or delayed action on a series of domestic proposals. And they came within an ace of tying the President's hands in foreign affairs through the proposed "Bricker Amendment" that would have curbed the negotiation of executive agreements and limited the legal effect of treaties. By December 1953 Eisenhower was so vexed with Republicans in Congress that he contemplated forming a new third party.

Only the aid of the Democrats in both houses saved Ike from an almost total rout. In 1953 he was successful on 74 issues; Democratic votes accounted for 58 of his victories. The elections of 1954, in which the Democrats won a majority of one in the Senate and of 29 in the House, proved a blessing in disguise. Although during the campaign Eisenhower had warned that a Democratic victory could bring "a cold war of partisan politics," the Democratic Congress backed him on nearly 50 per cent of the issues it voted upon.

EISENHOWER'S concept of his office also affected his relations with Senator McCarthy. McCarthy quickly took advantage of Eisenhower's belief in the limited powers of the President to run roughshod over the executive branch. Some of Eisenhower's advisers, and much of the country, urged the President to do battle with McCarthy, but he refused. When McCarthy rampaged through the Administration's foreign affairs agencies, neither Eisenhower nor Dulles attempted to stop him. Indeed, Dulles named a McCarthyite as the State Department's security officer, refrained from making diplomatic appointments that might offend McCarthy and sacrificed State Department career officers who had aroused the animosity of right-wingers.

Alarmed by the fearful drop in morale in the Foreign Service, five highly respected retired career diplomats warned in a public letter that the effectiveness of the service was being destroyed; men of integrity had been dismissed, and those still serving were afraid to report the truth from abroad.

Dulles' acts won him no special treatment from McCarthy. The senator sent two youthful aides, Roy Cohn and G. David Schine, on an 18-day tour of Europe to unearth evidence of subversion in the overseas information program. By the time Cohn and Schine had concluded their whirlwind junket, they had made a laughingstock of themselves and of the United States government. Nonetheless, the State Department bowed to McCarthy's demands for the dismissal of men who had met the disfavor of his two aides.

By early 1954, McCarthy was after bigger game. When he directed his attention to the Army, Secretary Robert Stevens pursued a course similar to Dulles', and with as little benefit. When McCarthy insisted that there were "earmarks of dangerous espionage" in the Signal Corps at Fort Monmouth, New Jersey, Stevens obligingly suspended those the senator had accused, despite protests that the suspensions disrupted valuable work.

But McCarthy persisted. In January 1954 he focused on the inconsequential case of Major Irving Peress, a New York dental officer, who had received a routine promotion and an honorable discharge although he had refused to sign the Army loyalty certificate. The senator summoned Army officials, including Brigadier General Ralph Zwicker, to a subcommittee hearing. When Zwicker refused to reveal certain privileged information, McCarthy stormed: "You are a disgrace to the uniform. You're shielding Communist conspirators. . . . You're not fit to be an officer. You're ignorant."

At this point, furious at such treatment of an esteemed general, Stevens ordered two other officers not to go before the subcommittee. McCarthy called Stevens an "awful dupe" and ordered the Secretary himself to appear before him. Stevens went, determined to read a strong statement. Instead he consented to a "Memorandum of Agreement," which was an unmistakable triumph for McCarthy. The Army had been humiliated.

Now the Administration, at long last, decided to take a stand. On March 11, 1954, the Army charged that McCarthy and his staff had sought to gain preferential treatment for Private G. David Schine, who had been drafted soon after the Cohn-Schine tour. McCarthy retorted that the Army was using Schine as a "hostage" to halt the probe of Fort Monmouth. Four days later the subcommittee voted to investigate the Army before television cameras.

The television tribunal proved the undoing of McCarthy. The senator met his match in his subcommittee opponent, Senator John McClellan, and even more in the Army's counsel, Joseph Welch, a scholarly, soft-spoken Boston attorney. The televised hearings enabled many people to see McCarthy in operation for the first time: to watch him bully witnesses, make baseless insinuations and indulge in self-serving interruptions in his sarcastic voice.

There was one special moment when, with startling suddenness, the character of the senator was exposed. On June 9, 1954, McCarthy broke into Welch's questioning with a gratuitous and irrelevant assault on a young member of Welch's law firm who, he charged, had once belonged to the National Lawyers Guild, which was alleged to have Communist ties. For the first time, Welch himself seemed to understand the full infamy of McCarthy's methods. His face taut with anger, the lawyer turned to McCarthy and cried: "Until this moment, Senator, I think I never really gauged your cruelty or your recklessness. . . . I like to think I am a gentle man, but your forgiveness will have to come from someone other than me. . . . Have you no sense of decency, sir, at long last? Have you left no sense of decency?"

As Welch finished, there was a hush; then, in violation of all the rules of decorum in the Senate Caucus Room, the audience burst into applause. Press photographers laid down their cameras to join in the clapping. In the Senate Caucus Room, shunned by reporters and spectators, McCarthy spread out his hands in genuine bewilderment and asked what he had done wrong.

THROUGHOUT the McCarthy years, the Senate, with a few notable exceptions, had played an inglorious role. Now that McCarthy's fortunes were declining, the senators belatedly began to act. They voted to form a select committee to consider a motion by Senator Flanders of Vermont to censure McCarthy for his actions. After a bitter debate, the Senate softened the terms of the resolution and voted 67-22 to condemn rather than censure the senator's methods.

George Humphrey, head of the Treasury Department in Eisenhower's Cabinet, was a brilliant businessman. This Midwestern conservative (his mother spelled Roosevelt with a small r) became a top executive with the M. A. Hanna Company. "He would fire his own grandmother if she wasn't doing a good job," an associate said, "but he'd put her on a pension."

Americans remitted their record-smashing 1951 taxes with a helpless shrug. The boss of a strip-tease joint complained that his girls were being taxed "as if they could strip forever." One cynic wrote: "One score and 19 years ago, our fathers brought forth upon this nation a new tax, conceived in desperation and dedicated to the proposition that all men are fair game."

The vote ignored the real issues—McCarthy was castigated not for reckless accusations or for assaults on men's rights but for offenses against the decorum of the Senate—but it marked the end of McCarthyism.

When the 1954 elections gave the Democrats a majority of one in the Senate, McCarthy lost his chairmanship of the Permanent Investigations Subcommittee. By 1956 he had fallen so far out of sight that he did not attend his party's national convention. On May 2, 1957, he died of "acute hepatitic failure," his force largely spent, his name a symbol for an episode in American history remembered with guilt. In his entire anti-Communist crusade he had not been responsible for rooting a single Communist out of any sensitive agency or for a single constructive piece of legislation.

The effects of McCarthyism survived McCarthy, particularly in the field of foreign policy. In this area the Eisenhower Administration was in a difficult position from the outset, caught between its desire to pursue a middle course and its promise to develop a dynamic new program. Secretary of State Dulles brought an internationalist outlook to his post. Yet he was concerned over the size of the nation's burgeoning military establishment and over the heavy burden of taxation requested to support foreign commitments.

Impatient with containment—"treadmill policies which, at best, might perhaps keep us in the same place until we drop exhausted"—Dulles wanted to seize the initiative. First of all he proposed giving official support to the "liberation" of the captive peoples behind the Iron Curtain. The satellites were to be liberated not by force but "by intelligent care" and by the intensity of human indignation. Those who minimized the power of moral pressure and propaganda, he claimed, "just do not know what they are talking about."

DULLES placed no faith in the concept of limited war. On January 12, 1954, he announced that henceforth America would depend less on local defense and more on "the deterrent of massive retaliatory power." Dulles' speech, noted Merlo Pusey, a historian friendly to the Administration, marked "the zenith of the cold war." The flaw in the massive-retaliation doctrine, protested political scientist Henry Kissinger, was that it turned every dispute into an occasion for a war of nuclear annihilation.

In keeping with the policy of massive retaliation, the Eisenhower Administration had taken what was called a "New Look" at defense spending. Twice it slashed the budget recommended by the Joint Chiefs of Staff. The idea was to reduce costly ground forces and rely instead on nuclear weapons and a large Air Force to deliver them. Despite the cutbacks, the Administration claimed the United States was getting greater security—in the expression of the period, "a bigger bang for a buck."

All of these Eisenhower programs—liberation, massive retaliation, the New Look—appeared to spell out a bold departure from the policy of containment and moderation. In practice they were much more modest, in part because some of the very people who disliked containment also wanted him to bring peace and even a withdrawal from international obligations. Eisenhower's election had owed less to his proposals for new initiatives in world affairs than to dismay over the fighting and casualties in Korea.

Even before taking office, Eisenhower fulfilled his pledge to go to Korea. After his inspection he conceded: "We have no panaceas." He rejected the MacArthur policy of risking total war to achieve total victory and determined instead on carrying out the Truman policy of negotiation and containment. On March 5, 1953, Stalin died, raising the possibility of a thaw in the Cold War. Three weeks later the Communists in Korea suddenly eased their demands, and on July 27 a cease-fire agreement was signed at Panmunjom. The agreement was, in fact, an armed truce with the peninsula divided along the battle line which roughly approximated the 38th Parallel. The U.N. returned more than 75,000 North Korean and Red Chinese prisoners, but it held to the principle that had long held up the negotiations—that no prisoner was to be forcibly repatriated. In all, the U.N. got back 3,746 Americans, together with some 9,000 prisoners of other nationalities, most of them South Koreans. Some 22,000 North Koreans and Chinese captured by U.N. forces refused repatriation; 21 Americans and 326 others chose to remain with the Communists.

I N securing a cease-fire in Korea, the President had set the pattern for the rest of his years in office: Warlike rhetoric would give way to deeds of peace. Such was the case in Indochina. Since 1946 the French rulers of that colony had been fighting the Communist leader Ho Chi Minh. Since the war was extremely unpopular in France, the United States had met much of the expense. In the spring of 1954 the French position became critical. Red forces besieged a French and Indochinese army at the vital fortress of Dien Bien Phu. Dulles feared that if Indochina went under, the United States defense perimeter might be forced back as far south as Australia; Richard Nixon asserted: "It is impossible to lay down arms until victory is completely won." Nevertheless, Dien Bien Phu fell without armed intervention by America. In July at Geneva, Indochina was divided, with the northern sector going to the Communists.

In an attempt to salvage something from the Indochina disaster, Dulles put together a Southeast Asia Treaty Organization in September 1954 to contain Communist expansion. But SEATO was a fragile reed. The terms of peace denied the new Indochinese nations the right to participate, and several important Asian states, including India and Indonesia, refused to join. The only nations in or near Asia to join SEATO, other than Pakistan and Thailand, were countries with which the United States already had security pacts: Australia, New Zealand and the Philippines, an independent republic since 1946.

That same month, a new crisis was developing that would demonstrate the precariousness of America's Far Eastern policy. In 1950, to help keep the Korean War from spreading beyond the peninsula, the Truman Administration had sent the U.S. Seventh Fleet into the Formosa Strait to act as a barrier between Red China and the Nationalist island of Formosa (Taiwan). This act had been criticized by Republicans who wanted to encourage Chiang Kai-shek to invade the mainland. Once in office, Eisenhower had rescinded part of Truman's order, thus "unleashing" Chiang to attack the Communists. The fact is, the Nationalists were not strong enough to invade, but Eisenhower's act encouraged Chiang to garrison or reinforce some small islands near the Chinese coast—Quemoy, Matsu and the Tachens—as possible bases for assaults on the mainland. In September 1954, in response to Communist shelling of the islands, Chiang's planes raided Amoy on the mainland. Suddenly America's determination to support Chiang threatened to involve it—and the rest of the world—in a nuclear war with Red China.

Congress granted Eisenhower authority to use armed force to repel any Red

"How deep do you think it goes?"   Mar. '54

When "dynamic doldrums" struck the American economy in 1953, the Administration was embarrassed. Above, recession-spelunker Eisenhower, as he anxiously peers into the recesses of the cavern, asks the elephant's advice. While some Republicans had denied the existence of a recession, others later claimed credit when it ended— hence the elephant's boast (below).

"It never existed—and I killed it"   Jul. '54

Chinese attack in the strait, but the Administration indicated it would not defend the offshore islands unless they were assaulted as part of a larger operation to seize Formosa. Nevertheless the situation in the strait remained explosive.

The tension over Quemoy and Matsu seemed part of a pattern in Dulles' handling of foreign affairs. "The ability to get to the verge without getting into the war is the necessary art," he explained. If "you are scared to go to the brink, you are lost. We've had to look it square in the face—on the question of enlarging the Korean War, on the question of getting into the Indochina war, on the question of Formosa. We walked to the brink and we looked it in the face. We took strong action."

This statement created a furor. Critics vociferously challenged the historical accuracy of Dulles' version of these incidents. They also questioned the soundness of a policy of what immediately became known as "brinkmanship" in a world of nuclear terror—a terror given new dimensions by continuing technological developments. In August 1953 the Russians detonated a hydrogen bomb. In the spring of 1954 the United States exploded a bomb one hundred times as destructive as any previous man-made explosion.

A T the same time, a change in Russian policy suggested the possibility of easing tensions. Symbolic of the new turn was the Soviet Union's agreement in May 1955 to a peace treaty that made Austria a neutral state and terminated the long four-power military occupation there.

In July 1955 the heads of the United States, Russia, Great Britain and France met at Geneva in a summit conference that seemed permeated with good feeling. "The United States will never take part in an aggressive war," President Eisenhower told Soviet Premier Nikolai Bulganin. "Mr. President, we believe that statement," Bulganin responded. During the conference Eisenhower—who had advanced an "atoms for peace" plan to a U.N. session in December 1953 in the hope of turning nuclear power to peaceful uses—made a dramatic proposal. He suggested that the United States and the U.S.S.R. give each other complete blueprints of their military establishments and provide facilities for mutual aerial reconnaissance of military installations.

Nothing came of Eisenhower's suggestion, but he exuded such warmth and friendliness that it was impossible for anyone to depict him as a warmonger bent on world conquest. The Geneva parley did little save defer all the hard questions to a subsequent meeting of foreign ministers to be held that fall. But for the moment, Geneva was a brilliant personal triumph for the President.

In the summer of 1955, Eisenhower was at the height of his popularity. A national poll reported that 60 per cent of Democratic voters wanted him as their own candidate. The adulation of Ike rested on more than trust in him as a man of peace. He was also a promoter of domestic tranquility. The partisanship of the late Truman years had been mitigated, the harshness of the McCarthy time had been tempered. The force of his personality and his refusal to agitate issues had helped dissipate the rancor of 1952. "Everybody ought to be happy every day . . ." Eisenhower is reported to have said once. "Play hard, have fun doing it, and despise wickedness."

There was a new spirit of moderation in the United States. In part it resulted from the Eisenhower influence, in part from a number of social changes that had occurred in the postwar decade. One of these was the growth of the

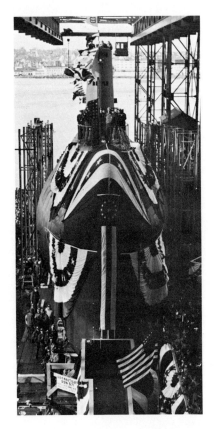

The submarine "Nautilus," the world's first atomic ship and sixth U.S. naval vessel of that name, awaits its launching in 1954—"a splash heard 'round the world." The sub cost about $55 million and later cruised some 70,000 miles— mostly submerged—on a single charge of uranium fuel. Among its amenities: a movie screen and a nuclear-powered soda pop machine.

managerial-professional class. In 1956 government statistics indicated that, for the first time, fewer Americans were producing things than were engaged in middle-class occupations.

As workers moved up into the middle class, or as the fortunes of the lower middle class were enhanced, they fled the city. From 1950 to 1955, suburbs grew seven times as fast as the central cities. The Republicans were especially strong in this commuter country. In New York's suburbs the G.O.P. polled 70 per cent of the 1952 ballots for President.

In the world of the new middle class, less value was placed on individual achievement, more on a man's capacity to adapt to the standards of the group. The suburban-dweller characteristically was interested not in conquering new worlds but in attending to his own family, garden and home. "A sleeping sickness is spreading among the women of the land," complained Fannie Hurst. "They are retrogressing into . . . that thing known as the Home."

The sense of well-being owed much to the speedy recovery from the recession that had occurred during Eisenhower's early months in office. In September 1955 steel production climbed to 96 per cent of capacity; the continuing migration westward produced a remarkable growth on the Pacific Coast; the construction of the St. Lawrence Seaway brought ocean-going vessels to Chicago and Duluth and promised a bonanza for the Midwest.

The American worker rejoiced in record employment and the highest living standard ever. In 1955, under the pace-setting Walter Reuther, auto workers won from Ford an agreement to receive a substantial proportion of their wages in the first months of unemployment—in effect a partially guaranteed annual wage. Other employers followed suit. In December 1955 the American Federation of Labor and the Congress of Industrial Organizations merged as the AFL-CIO, adding new strength to the union movement.

On September 24, 1955, the President, while vacationing in Denver, suffered a heart attack of "moderate" severity. Americans followed every detail of the President's heartbeat, respiratory rate and intestinal tone. For weeks the President was unable to assume the burdens of office, and a "team" headed by Vice President Nixon in Washington and Sherman Adams at Lowry Air Force Base in Denver carried out some of the President's functions.

The illness seemed certain to limit Eisenhower to a single term of office. But Ike made a remarkable recovery. After a panel of doctors told reporters in February 1956 that the scar on the President's heart muscle had healed, he announced that he would run for a second term. Then in June 1956, he was stricken again—this time with an intestinal inflammation. He was operated on. Soon his doctors were announcing that his health was as good as ever.

W ITH its candidates decided on in advance (although Harold Stassen made an abortive attempt to keep Nixon off the ticket), the Republican convention of 1956 went through its paces like a jaded company of actors. Even though Eisenhower's re-election seemed certain, the Democratic convention was more spirited. Competition for the Democratic nomination was stiff; Stevenson had to campaign vigorously in the primaries to defeat a strong bid by Estes Kefauver, and then had to fight off a new challenge in the convention from New York's Governor W. Averell Harriman, who was sponsored by Truman.

After winning the nomination, Stevenson announced, surprisingly, that he was leaving the choice of his running mate to the delegates. Kefauver was

Senator Ralph Flanders of Vermont, formerly an engineer and Federal Reserve Bank president, moved to censure his fellow Republican, Senator McCarthy, in 1954. Although his opponent accused him of "senility," Flanders —who once said he was "anti-pink, antimink and antistink"— stuck to his guns. The Senate supported Flanders; McCarthy was never again a major political force.

nominated, but only after turning back an unexpectedly strong attempt by the young senator from Massachusetts, John F. Kennedy. Kennedy's showing suggested that for the first time since 1928 the party might be willing to name a Catholic candidate for national office—perhaps even for the presidency.

In the 1956 campaign, both candidates appeared before the country as men of moderation. But Stevenson raised two dramatic new issues. He recommended giving "prompt and earnest consideration to stopping further tests of the hydrogen bomb," and he suggested "that within the foreseeable future we can maintain the military forces we need without the draft."

In pressing these points Stevenson added greatly to Eisenhower's political advantage. To some, Stevenson's position indicated that he was "soft on Communism"; others felt helpless to judge the technical issues involved. Forced to choose between Stevenson's judgment and that of General Eisenhower on what appeared to be military questions, the nation leaned toward the successful soldier. But in the very last week of the campaign, issues arose over which neither candidate had the slightest control.

I N late February 1956 Russian leader Nikita Khrushchev had shocked a secret meeting of Russian Communist functionaries by denouncing Stalin as a monstrous tyrant. The Russian policy of de-Stalinization that followed encouraged Soviet satellites to a show of independence. By October 19, Polish Communists were setting up a new regime modeled on the independent, nationalistic Communism established by Tito in Yugoslavia. Even though Khrushchev flew to Warsaw and threatened suppression by force, the Polish Communists stood up to him. Soviet troops and tanks, moving toward Warsaw, halted before reaching the city, and the Poles won a measure of autonomy. They named the Titoist Wladyslaw Gomulka as chief of their party and voted to expel the Soviet marshal, Konstantin Rokossovsky.

Even more dramatic was the uprising in Hungary. In the last weeks of October the Hungarians overturned their government and brought back ex-Premier Imre Nagy, who promised free elections. The Red army departed Budapest on October 30. For a few days the world thrilled to the thought that the tyranny behind the Iron Curtain was dissolving. But on November 4 the Russian army returned to crush the revolution ruthlessly.

The events in Hungary shattered any illusion that the U.S.S.R. headed an idealistic "people's movement." They also destroyed the pretensions of Dulles' liberation policy. The United States watched helplessly while the courageous Hungarian uprising was crushed. Some Europeans even accused America of encouraging a revolt which it had no intention of supporting.

The same week that the Hungarian revolt was wiped out, the Administration's program to stabilize the Middle East collapsed. In the Middle East there were no easy choices. In that seething region the United States was attempting to maintain the friendship of all the parties: the Arab nations; Britain and France, the imperial powers in the region; and Israel. The entire region was eyed hungrily by the Russians; to forestall any Soviet move, Dulles in 1955 promoted the Baghdad Pact, which joined the northern Moslem bloc—Turkey, Iran, Iraq and Pakistan—to the Western defense system. But when the pact awakened resentment through a vast area from India (hostile to Pakistan) to Egypt (which saw its pre-eminence in the Arab world jeopardized), the United States itself refrained from joining the alliance.

Quemoy and Matsu, two bleak and undesirable islands in the Formosa Strait, became a center of world attention as early as 1949. The Chinese Communists coveted the islands as "stepping stones to Formosa" (above). But even more, they wanted to eject the Nationalists, who threatened to use the islands as bases for attacking the mainland, just a few miles away.

Egypt, strategically located, constituted a special problem. To win Egypt's friendship, the United States urged that the British evacuate the Sudan. Americans also offered to help construct the mammoth Aswan Dam to harness the power of the Nile. Still Cairo showed no sign of being any better disposed to the West. Egypt bought arms from the U.S.S.R., stepped up border raids on Israel, a nation for which Americans felt great sympathy, and recognized Red China. Then Dulles decided to teach Egyptian leader Gamal Abdel Nasser a lesson. He withdrew the American offer on the Aswan Dam.

Outraged, Nasser struck back. On the fourth anniversary of the Egyptian revolution he announced that he had nationalized the Suez Canal. The canal, previously operated by a company controlled by Anglo-French stockholders, had been open to vessels of all nations. Now Nasser closed it to the Israelis and held other users at his mercy.

In the final week of the 1956 election campaign in America, the Middle East crisis erupted in war. On October 29, Israel invaded Egypt for the announced purpose of destroying bases from which the Egyptians had launched their border raids. Two days later Britain and France intervened to drive the Egyptians out of the Suez zone. Within a few days Russia had threatened Britain and France with reprisals unless they withdrew.

Fearful that the Soviets might make good their threat, and angry at the British and French for their gunboat diplomacy, the United States joined with Russia in condemning the military intervention. Under this pressure Britain and France agreed to a cease-fire, and Israeli forces retired. After the cease-fire the American government took the lead in asking for withdrawal of Israeli troops and U.N. supervision of a cease-fire arrangement. In the end the Western alliance had been shaken; the power of the Soviet Union had been confirmed in a new part of the world; Nasser's prestige had been enhanced even though he had been drubbed in the field; and the United States had embittered the Israelis without winning the friendship of the Arabs.

Under ordinary circumstances, all these troubles might have made election difficulties for an incumbent administration. But the Republicans, who had been claiming that only Eisenhower guaranteed peace, now advanced the argument that only the President could be trusted in a time of crisis.

At 7:30 p.m. on election night came disheartening news for the Democrats. Bridgeport, Connecticut, a Democratic factory town, had gone for Eisenhower by a thumping 19,000 votes. Minutes later New Haven, which had never voted for a Republican presidential candidate, gave Eisenhower a 17,000 plurality. It was clear immediately that not only would Ike win—but he would win by a landslide. With 35.6 million votes, the President swept 41 states with an electoral vote of 457 and a popular percentage of 57.4. But the elections had one surprising feature: The Democrats continued to control both houses of Congress, the Senate by two votes, the House by 32.

No one knew quite how to interpret the curious outcome of the election. Of Eisenhower's popularity, there could be no doubt. But what was one to make of the Democratic triumph in Congress? The country, some concluded, wanted both peace and prosperity. It trusted the President to preserve peace and the Democrats to forestall hard times. One thing was clear: Eisenhower had failed to rebuild the Republican party into an instrumentality that could command the support of the nation.

The public generally regarded John Foster Dulles as a remote sort of grand old man who juggled the world in his powerful hands. A New York television audience was startled, then, when comedienne Carol Burnett sang that she was "on fire with desire for John Foster Dulles." An aide to the Secretary of State quickly sent a telegram saying Dulles was "very amused."

RACIAL CRISIS in postwar America is starkly etched as Martin Luther King Jr. (center) is arrested by the police chief of Albany, Georgia, in 1962. King, a leader of the Negro civil rights movement, was sent to jail for staging a demonstration in that city.

Dilemmas of growth and wealth

FOR all of their native optimism, Americans in the 1950s were sobered by perplexing paradoxes that accompanied the country's spectacular postwar growth. Between 1945 and 1960 the Gross National Product more than doubled, reaching $503 billion, yet America felt the tremors of recession. In that period the average per capita income rose from $1,177 to $2,215 a year, but the rise in the cost of living wiped out much of the gain; and while the number of jobholders jumped from 52.8 million to 70.6 million, unemployment climbed from 2.5 per cent in 1953 to about 6 per cent for most of the following decade. There were chronically sick sectors of the economy: agriculture and the railroads, whose well-being depended on federal aid; the coal industry, many of whose miners had been reduced to government wards by automation and loss of markets; the 20 million Negro citizens who, as one of their most eloquent spokesmen, Martin Luther King (above), declared, lived "on a lonely island of poverty in the midst of a vast ocean of material prosperity."

Big government, big industry, big labor—all struggled to cope with the problems of an economy that was as complex as it was dynamic. The individual, dwarfed and often bewildered by a vast, impersonal society, went his way with seeming self-confidence. Americans moved within their own country, went abroad for business and pleasure. But anxiety persisted, and they sought reassurance in churchgoing, release in watching television, miraculous answers in education. Many realized that not only had their lives changed—there was a strange new difference in the nature of change itself.

INDUSTRIAL PROGRESS is typified by this huge West Virginia plant, which in spite of automation employed 10,000 in chemical research, development and production.

Watching white youths play, Negro children in Mobile, Alabama, stand wistfully outside a playground shut off to them by segregation.

"Freedom *now!*": The Negro's drive for full equality

IN a speech on June 11, 1963, President John F. Kennedy summed up the inequities that had fired the most powerful social movement in postwar America—the drive of Negroes for full equality. A Negro baby born anywhere in the United States, said Kennedy, "has about one-half as much chance of completing high school as a white baby . . . one-third as much chance of becoming a professional man, twice as much chance of becoming unemployed, about one-seventh as much chance of earning ten thousand dollars a year, a life expectancy which is seven years shorter, and the prospects of earning only half as much."

Nine years earlier the Supreme Court had declared against segregated public schools. Building on this legal substructure, Negroes began nationwide campaigns to secure their constitutional guarantees. In the South they struggled against disfranchisement imposed upon them by gerrymandering, "interpretation" and "literacy" tests; and they brought their increasing purchasing power to

bear in boycotts. Joined by white students and clergymen, they staged nonviolent sit-ins and freedom rides.

In the North, Negroes contended with problems far more subtle but no less difficult—the problems of *de facto* segregation. Concentrated into "black ghettos," Negro families were victimized by slum landlords, condemned to the use of inferior schools and denied consideration for better jobs. Even those Negroes who could afford comfortable homes were hard put to find decent ones. Even among white liberals who supported civil liberties, some resisted the influx of Negro families into their neighborhoods in order "to protect their property values."

Despite the profound changes that their demands entailed, most Negroes would no longer accept gradual attainment of integration or tolerate any concomitants of second-class citizenship. "Freedom *now!*" became their slogan. The Reverend Martin Luther King Jr. warned that "there will be neither rest nor tranquillity" in America until all Negro citizens received full rights.

Arguing for the preservation of Southern traditions, a speaker endorses segregation at a labor union rally in Birmingham, Alabama.

NORTHERN RACISM, threatening violence to new Negro tenants *(in window in background)*, keeps Chicago policemen on night duty around a campfire in the fall of 1953. For more than three years police maintained this vigil at the Trumbull Park project.

A UNIQUE SYNAGOGUE in Elkins Park, Pennsylvania, rises to a high glass roof. The architect was Frank Lloyd Wright.

FLOODLIT ALTAR of a Roman Catholic church in St. Louis is backed by a striking mural representing the Apostles' Creed.

New buildings for worship, a new search for faith

AMERICA in the '50s witnessed a great resurgence of religious activity. According to estimates, total church membership jumped from 86.8 million to 114.4 million. Building programs raised countless new houses of worship, many daringly modern in design *(above)*. Evangelists thrived; in 15 weeks in 1957 Billy Graham *(right)* preached to some two million in New York.

Numerous churchmen felt that the renascence lacked depth and attributed it to social strivings or fear of war. An Episcopal bishop suggested that in the nuclear age, God had become "a sort of tranquilizer pill to a populace keeping a wary eye on the Sword of Damocles." Others noted that new churches serving the heavy postwar migration to the suburbs largely owed their membership gains to losses by city congregations.

By the early 1960s enrollment in many religious bodies had begun lagging behind the rate of population growth. Far from being disheartened by this trend, some thoughtful clerics firmly believed that it signaled a more profound revival—a yearning for the rich ceremony of the past, a search for new values. A Baptist pastor declared: "The church is moving inward . . . to rediscover the reality that lies beneath the outward structure."

A CALL TO WORSHIP by Billy Graham (arms outstretched) brings believers surging down the aisles of New York's Madison Square Garden to make a "decision for Christ."

A pilot from the U.S. base at Thule, Greenland, tests survival methods in an igloo.

An American agriculturist in Cambodia inspects

A Navy officer relaxes in his family's home in Japan. Americans in the Far East in 1957 included 205,000 servicemen, 92,000 dependents.

ramie plants, which yield textile fiber. Including such technical assistance, U.S. aid to 23 Asian countries amounted to $1.8 billion in 1957.

A host of Americans working and traveling abroad

IN the postwar world, more Americans than ever before were living and traveling abroad. The year 1957, for example, saw 599,000 servicemen based in 21 countries, and with them were 413,000 dependents. As part of U.S. commitments to underdeveloped nations, thousands of American technical experts were scattered to the far corners of the globe. Government employees, students and educators added 164,000 to the Americans abroad. American investments in foreign business, which reached $37 billion in 1957 (and continued to increase by about four billion dollars a year), brought a commensurate rise in the number of Americans working and visiting overseas on business. They built plants in the neat French countryside, prospected for oil in frigid Tierra del Fuego, made toothpaste in steaming Bombay.

The crowning statistic, which brought the 1957 total of American trips abroad to 6.5 million, was supplied by the tourist. As casually as they once drove to a shore resort, wage earners of modest means hopped jet planes for vacations abroad. And as they "did" European capitals and whole countries in a few days, they left in their wake citizens of the older nations dazed by the eagerness, the energy and the free spending of the Americans.

IN VENEZUELA the American foreman of an oil rig greets a native carrying a drill bit. Thousands of U.S. workers were lured to South America by high wages and hardy frontier life.

119

In agriculture: vexing surpluses, vanishing farmers

AMERICA'S farmer, the bellwether of prosperity until the 1870s but the sick man of the economy after 1920, suffered a sharp decline in the 1950s. Agriculture was suffering from headlong scientific progress. Between the late '40s and 1960, the average wheat yield per acre jumped from 16.9 bushels to 26.2 bushels, while the acres harvested decreased from 70.3 million to 51.9 million. The number of farms, six million in 1945, shrank to 3.9 million by 1960; and in the same period workers in agriculture declined from 8.6 million to 5.7 million. In sum, bigger and bigger harvests were being wrung from less and less land; and on fewer but larger farms, machines and improved agricultural techniques were eliminating the farm hand—and the small farmer.

Those farmers who survived the transition to large-scale mechanized agriculture seemed to be earning more than ever before: Farm income rose from $22.4 billion in 1945 to $34.7 billion in 1960. But farmers depended for their profit on huge production and government aid, which cost some four billion dollars a year by 1960 (including about one million a day for storing the vast surpluses that the price-support program helped to build). Actually the income of many farmers decreased as their production increased. For the thousands of farm families who were forced to leave their home acres and to find new work, it was small consolation that America's farm problem was one of plenty rather than scarcity.

UNLOADING COTTON, a mechanical picker empties its huge hopper from the back of a tractor. The machine, a model introduced around 1950, picked as much cotton as seven field hands.

MODERN COMBINES, harvesting wheat (*opposite*) in Oklahoma, cut a continuous swath inward to the center of huge squares. At top right a truck waits to carry off the grain.

SCIENTIFIC FEEDING fattens the Hereford cattle seen in this wide-angle view of a Colorado pen. Cash sales of cattle increased sharply from $1.4 billion in 1940 to $7.4 billion in 1960.

TELEVISION STUDENTS in a California university shoot a two-man drama and watch it on monitors in the foreground. Graduates of such classes often landed television or movie jobs.

Watching in a bar, avid viewers follow a program of election returns.

LAVISH TRAPPINGS for an Ed Sullivan show include a knight on horseback, girls in mink. The camera focuses on host Sullivan, a perennial leader in the ratings, and singer Eartha Kitt.

Comedies, quizzes, "singing cough drops"

TELEVISION meant free shows in the home. Responding to this irresistible appeal, Americans bought some 76 million sets between 1945 and 1960. Television swept America, revolutionizing habits and customs.

While still in its infancy, the new medium came under heavy attack. Serious critics deplored its irresponsible programing—hour after banal hour of heavy-handed comedy, stereotyped Westerns, grandiose variety shows, overblown quizzes. To buttress complaints that television had sold its soul to the advertisers, one observer described the persistent commercials as a "panorama of flying beer bottles, zooming candy bars . . . singing cough drops and animated coffee cups." Educators and civic officials accused producers of dramatizing robberies and violence so realistically that many shows became blueprints for juvenile crime.

But by the '60s television was being reappraised. Critics were forced to acknowledge the excellence of its documentaries and political and sports coverage. Sociologists, who at first surmised that television would strengthen the weakening family unit, were appalled by families whose members watched the screen for hours without exchanging a word. At the same time, the doomsayers who had decried sponsors' insistence on catering to the lowest possible denominator saw signs that the tastes of a discerning minority were being considered.

Television reshaped political campaigns with its coverage of such events as nominating conventions and the Kennedy-Nixon debates in 1960.

Astronaut John H. Glenn Jr.

Second thoughts on the threshold of the space age

Lifting off at Cape Canaveral early in 1962, Lieutenant Colonel John Glenn begins his historic flight in a capsule at the nose of an Atlas rocket.

AT precisely 9:47 a.m. on February 20, 1962, the tremendous endeavors of science, industry and government combined climactically to launch the rocket *(below)* that put the first American astronaut *(left)* into orbit. Overjoyed at the triumphant thrust into space, the nation plunged confidently into an all-out race with the Soviet Union to land the first man on the moon.

But as America's program of space exploration proceeded, cautionary questions were raised. Were there not real dangers in a national prosperity artificially stimulated by vast expenditures on space hardware? Might not some of these billions be spent more productively on aid to education or conquering disease? How much more was the taxpayer willing to spend to put an American on the moon in 1970 instead of, say, 1973?

For the first time in its history, the wealthiest nation on earth was forced to pause and consciously weigh its national prestige against the current price of progress.

Weightless for 4.7 hours, Glenn made three orbits 99 to 162 miles above the earth, then he came down safely in the Atlantic near the Bahamas.

6. A NATION IN SEARCH OF A GOAL

Dᴜʀɪɴɢ his second term in office, Dwight Eisenhower faced new challenges. In his first four years, he had conciliated a politically divided nation. Now something more was expected of him: that he capitalize on his enormous popularity to help the country solve problems too long postponed. The pressure of the population explosion was being felt increasingly in schools, hospitals and housing. The Negro's mounting cry for equality made it clear that token integration would no longer suffice. To meet the competition of the Communist world, the nation would require a more creative foreign policy and a firmer sense of national purpose.

By the fall of 1952 Soviet policy had begun to move in a new direction. By espousing anticolonialism, it aimed to diminish the power of the West. It began to rely more on economic and political penetration than on military force or subversion. Most important, the Russians showed signs of believing that although Communism would ultimately triumph over capitalism, it might well do so through peaceful competition rather than war.

Crucial to the revised Soviet strategy was the U.S.S.R.'s determination to show that it was the world's leader in technological, economic and scientific development. It sought to prove its boast in two ways: by outpacing America's rate of industrial growth and, in a more spectacular fashion, by taking the lead in the development of rockets and missiles. In 1955 James R. Killian Jr., president of the Massachusetts Institute of Technology, headed

MARTYRED PRESIDENT, John F. Kennedy, first Chief
Executive to be born in the 20th Century, sits at his desk
in the picture he chose as his official color photograph.

a committee of scientists that concluded that the Soviet Union was overtaking the United States and would soon have "a decided superiority in intercontinental ballistic missiles."

Also deeply involved in the struggle for the allegiance of the new nations of Africa and Asia was a troublesome American domestic issue: civil rights. A country which claimed to speak to the world as the champion of liberty and justice could not continue to deny fundamental rights to its own citizens.

For more than a half century, racial discrimination in the United States had been sustained by court rulings based on an 1896 verdict of the Supreme Court; *Plessy vs. Ferguson* had held that segregation did not violate the 14th Amendment so long as facilities which were separate were also equal. In May 1954 the Supreme Court handed down a historic decision. In *Brown vs. Board of Education of Topeka*, it abandoned the Plessy doctrine and ruled unanimously that segregation in the public schools was unconstitutional. "Separate educational facilities," said Chief Justice Earl Warren, "are inherently unequal." In a subsequent decision, the Court ruled that public-school integration should be pursued "with all deliberate speed."

Partial desegregation of the schools was speedily achieved in some border states, but in the Deep South and in Virginia, resistance was adamant, especially in those areas where the militantly segregationist White Citizens' Councils emerged. In Tennessee John Kasper, a fanatical segregationist from New Jersey, stirred up an orgy of violence. Rope in hand, talking of dynamite, Kasper told a Nashville crowd: "When they fool with the white race they're fooling with the strongest race in the world, the most bloodthirsty race in the world." Early the next day a dynamite blast shattered a wing of the Hattie Cotton Elementary School, where a five-year-old Negro girl had registered the day before.

If the Court's decision was to be enforced, it had to be made clear that the verdict was the law of the land, not merely a caprice of nine men. The President was urged to take action to indicate he supported the Court's ruling as a significant stride forward in democracy. He declined to do so.

At the beginning of Eisenhower's second term, three years after the Court's decision, not a single child in the Deep South attended a desegregated school. At last a federal court in 1956 ordered Little Rock, Arkansas, to start integration in the 1957-1958 school year. Little Rock seemed an excellent choice. "Jim Crow"—segregated seating—had disappeared on the city's buses, the city had Negro policemen and its school board was well disposed toward at least token integration. The University of Arkansas had been desegregated since 1948, and several communities in the northern part of the state had integrated their schools without opposition from the state's governor, Orval Faubus.

On Monday night, September 2, 1957, as plans were proceeding for the admission of nine Negro students to Little Rock's Central High School the next morning, Faubus abruptly dispatched a unit of the state National Guard to the school. An hour later he told a television audience that he was acting to forestall violence. Outraged white citizens, he claimed, were converging on Little Rock, and the city's stores were selling out of knives, "mostly to Negro youths."

The mayor, the superintendent of schools, the police chief and the F.B.I.

In 1960 Negro college students in the South began the "sit-in" aimed at "whites only" lunch counters, thus triggering a militant, massive campaign against segregation in the South. One writer pointed out that no one objected when Negroes and whites stood together—to buy groceries or pay bills. "It is only when the Negro 'sets' that the fur begins to fly," he concluded wryly.

all subsequently denied that there had been any signs of violence. But Faubus, who may have hoped that a racial crisis would improve his prospects for a third term, succeeded by his action and speeches in creating the very atmosphere of violence he professed to deplore. "The only effect of his action," Mayor Woodrow Wilson Mann declared, "is to create tensions where none existed." The next morning, on the advice of the school superintendent, none of the Negro children showed up at Central High School.

Alarmed by the consequences of Faubus' defiance of the federal courts, Representative Brooks Hays, an Arkansas moderate, persuaded the governor to telegraph the President requesting a meeting. Eisenhower agreed, and a Marine helicopter landed Faubus on the lawn of the President's vacation headquarters at Newport, Rhode Island. After the meeting, the governor appeared to have agreed to an early withdrawal of the troops. No sooner had Faubus returned to Little Rock, however, than he once more adopted a defiant stance. It required another federal court order to compel the governor to withdraw the Guardsmen and permit the Negro pupils to be admitted. But by now the threat of mob violence, once largely illusory, had become real. Without adequate force, there was no possibility that the children could attend school.

At that point Eisenhower federalized the National Guard and ordered a detachment of the 101st Airborne Division, a Regular Army unit, to Little Rock. At 5 a.m. on September 25, paratroopers stood with fixed bayonets at their posts ringing the school. At 9:25 an Army station wagon rolled up to the school and the nine Negro pupils were led inside.

The episode had dealt a heavy blow to America's prestige. When the French government sought to work out a solution to the painful Algerian civil war, a hard-core nationalist cried: "Why should the French have a bad conscience? It's not France that must use armed troops to put children into school." When a Ceylonese delegate to the U.N. denounced Soviet intervention in Hungary, a Bulgarian retorted: "Something worse could happen to you if you go to Little Rock."

President Eisenhower, who had been almost immune from censure in his first term, now encountered a barrage of criticism for the first time. The critics were Republicans and Democrats alike, and from every part of the country. The President, they cried, had permitted an explosive situation to erupt without doing anything to head it off. Two months earlier he had said: "I can't imagine any set of circumstances that would ever induce me to send federal troops." Now he had sent in the paratroopers. "The President," commented the New York *Times*, "did, belatedly and powerfully, what he might not have had to do at all if he had previously made his position unmistakably and publicly understood."

Eisenhower studiously avoided taking a position on the Supreme Court decision. He observed: "I have never said what I thought about the Supreme Court decision—I have never told a soul." He made a point of saying that he had ordered the troops in only because the sanctity of the courts was at stake, not because of "the segregation problem." It was not until 1963 that, as ex-President, Eisenhower finally announced that he considered the Court's desegregation decision "morally and legally correct."

In August 1957 Congress passed the first civil rights law in 82 years. To

Die-hard Southern segregationists, like this New Orleans woman (above), responded with rage to token integration of the public schools. Police in some towns met Negro demonstrators with electric cattle prods, vicious dogs and high-pressure hoses, thus encouraging extremists—"the duck-tailed, sideburned swaggerers, the rednecked hatemongers, the Ku Klux Klan."

A 1957 cartoon shows Uncle Sam —on the ground with his satellite program still on paper—bowled over by Russia's space accomplishments. After "Sputnik" the U.S. space agency was frequently the object of cynical stories. One told of a reporter who telephoned to ask about its program. "Sir, are you calling for information or with information?" was the reply.

afford some federal protection to Negroes wanting to vote, the measure established a Civil Rights Commission. A second act in 1960 authorized the appointment of federal referees to safeguard voting rights and stipulated that threatening violence to obstruct federal court orders was a crime. With the support of the able Attorney General, William Rogers, the Civil Rights Commission strove to use its powers to expand Negro suffrage.

Yet congressional action still was of small consequence. More significant in the long run was an episode in Montgomery, Alabama, on December 1, 1955. A middle-aged Negro seamstress, riding home from a day's work, refused to get up to give her seat to a white man. When she was arrested for defying the state's Jim Crow laws, Montgomery's Negroes began a boycott. Under the leadership of a young Negro minister, Dr. Martin Luther King Jr., who had been influenced by Gandhi, they employed passive resistance in a campaign to desegregate the city's buses. After 54 weeks the city and the bus company, nudged by a federal injunction, gave in.

The Montgomery bus boycott indicated a new militancy among Southern Negroes, particularly young Negroes. On February 1, 1960, four freshmen from a Negro college in North Carolina sat down at the segregated lunch counter at Woolworth's in downtown Greensboro; when the waitress refused to sell them a cup of coffee, they remained in their seats. In the next 18 months 70,000 Negroes and whites joined in sit-ins, wade-ins (at segregated pools and beaches), kneel-ins (in churches) and other movements to end the pattern of segregation. Other Negroes and whites took part in "freedom rides" to put an end to Jim Crow in interstate transportation. They made some progress, but patterns of segregation, in both North and South, continued to embarrass the United States. When the finance minister of Ghana bought orange juice at a Howard Johnson's restaurant near Dover, Delaware, he was not allowed to drink it on the premises because he was a Negro. No one doubted that the United States was changing its laws, but many questioned whether its customs were changing quickly enough.

TEN days after the President dispatched troops to Little Rock, America's complacency received a new jolt: The Soviet Union announced that it had launched the world's first successful artificial satellite into space. *Sputnik*, meaning "traveling companion," orbited the earth at 18,000 miles per hour at a height of up to 560 miles, emitting beeping coded signals. Its success indicated that the U.S.S.R. was far ahead of the United States in rocketry. At its most optimistic, the United States had hoped to launch a satellite some five months later and weighing less than one eighth as much as *Sputnik*.

Sputnik dealt a mighty blow at what one writer had called "the illusion of American omnipotence." The United States had been outstripped in the very area it was proudest of: technical know-how. The Soviets touted their achievement as proof of the superiority of their system; the uncommitted nations listened attentively.

The shock of *Sputnik* prompted a reassessment of America's intellectual life. United States schools were compared unfavorably (and often unfairly) to Soviet schools, and school boards began to revamp curricula to give more emphasis to science and mathematics. But the Administration responded to *Sputnik* with remarkable complacency. Rear Admiral Rawson Bennett, Chief of the Office of Naval Research, which was in charge of the lagging American satellite program, dismissed the Soviet satellite as a "hunk of iron almost anybody could launch." President Eisenhower, asked whether he proposed to appoint a science adviser, said, "I hadn't thought of that."

On November 3 the Administration had a rude awakening. That day the U.S.S.R. hurled into orbit the much heavier *Sputnik II*, an enormous satellite weighing more than six times as much as *Sputnik I*. Within it was a live dog. It was a stunning achievement, indicating a highly advanced state of rocketry. Within a week the Administration announced the appointment of James Killian as special assistant to the President for science and technology; at the same time it supplemented the Navy's satellite program with the Army's Jupiter-C test rocket.

The Navy's failure to make good with its Vanguard satellite program mortified most Americans. In early December reporters from foreign newspapers arrived at Cape Canaveral (later to be Cape Kennedy) in Florida to watch the United States send its first satellite into orbit, only to see one attempt postponed and another abort. The world press commented derisively.

On the last day of January 1958, gloom turned to rejoicing when, at Cape Canaveral, the Army, called in only 12 weeks earlier to save America's face, put the first United States satellite into orbit. As the Jupiter-C missile rose majestically from its launching pad, some reporters cheered. Still, the new *Explorer* satellite was much smaller than the Soviet version. As late as 1959 Khrushchev could jeer: "You send up oranges while we send up tons."

The gap between American and Soviet technical achievements was never so great as some feared, and the United States had already marked up some technical accomplishments of its own, notably its successful development of an atomic-powered submarine. Nevertheless the nation remained behind the U.S.S.R. in the development of vital intermediate and long-range missiles. The "missile gap" was to handicap considerably the conduct of foreign affairs in Eisenhower's second term.

Foreign policy during this period was concerned largely with efforts to win the support of the small nations of the world. Two weeks before the start of his second Administration, Eisenhower asked Congress for authority to use troops "to secure and protect the territorial integrity and political independence" of countries requesting aid against "overt armed aggression from any nation controlled by International Communism." This move was aimed specifically at the Middle East, but it failed to take into account the desire of most Middle Eastern nations for neutrality in the Cold War.

In 1955 Dulles had promoted the Baghdad Pact. Of the Arab states, only Iraq had joined—and a strong but submerged opposition to the pact had developed in that country. In July 1958 the pro-Western government of Iraq was overturned and its leaders slain. The rebellion was led by initially pro-Nasser elements, and it appeared to threaten the governments of Jordan and Lebanon. At Lebanon's request, Eisenhower immediately dispatched 9,000 Marines and paratroopers to that country. Britain sent forces to sustain the government of Jordan.

The Lebanon action precipitated an international crisis which brought the world very close to war. Khrushchev threatened to intervene, Mao made his voice heard, and Nasser attempted to play the Russians off against the West. In the end a U.N. resolution eased the immediate crisis, but there was

By the time the U.S. Atlas intercontinental missile became the fifth successful American satellite in 1958, the post-"Sputnik" gloom had lifted. Commenting on the use of an Atlas communications satellite to beam President Eisenhower's Christmas message back to earth, a visiting Russian scientist said: ". . . we haven't thought of doing anything like that yet."

little left of the Eisenhower policy. By the time the American troops were withdrawn, Lebanon had a neutralist president and prime minister, and for the time being both Nasser and the Soviets had enhanced their power in the Middle East.

While the American troops were deployed in Lebanon, a new crisis developed on the other side of the globe. On August 23, 1958, Red China began a major bombardment of Quemoy. Though the Joint Chiefs of Staff held that the offshore islands were not essential to the defense of Formosa, Dulles felt that any use of force by the Communists in the western Pacific was a menace to world order and that it was a "vital interest" of the United States to fight back.

A commemorative stamp, which used the same star motif as the Alaskan flag designed by an Indian child, marked the entry of the first state not contiguous to U.S. territory. The 49th state, rich in fur, fish, gold, oil and untapped resources, Alaska was bought from Russia in 1867 for two cents an acre.

ONCE again the world seemed to tremble on the brink of war. American warships escorted Chiang's transports to the three-mile limit off Quemoy; the Seventh Fleet, equipped with nuclear weapons, plied the Formosa Strait; Dulles suggested that the United States might bomb the Chinese mainland if Formosa or Quemoy were attacked or threatened. America's allies were deeply disturbed by this position, and Dulles received biting criticism at home. Senator Herbert Lehman declared that "not a single American life . . . should be sacrificed for the defense" of these islands.

On September 30 Dulles announced his willingness to encourage negotiation. He declared that the United States had "no commitment of any kind" to help Chiang back to the mainland and that any hopes for his return were "highly hypothetical." Eisenhower went even further; Chiang's buildup of troops on the islands, the President asserted, was "a thorn in the side of peace." After a three-day conference in Taipei, Dulles and Chiang issued a joint statement on October 23 in which Chiang renounced the use of force to regain control of the mainland of China.

As crises mounted—Little Rock, *Sputnik*, Lebanon, Quemoy—there was unusually severe criticism of the President, primarily on grounds that he seemed to be following a policy (as he himself put it) of "not making decisions until after the event reaches you." Political analyst Samuel Lubell found that even Ike's admirers were grumbling: "Things are in an uproar, but what is Eisenhower doing? All you read about is that he's playing golf. Who is running the country?" When Eisenhower took a 10-day vacation trip to Georgia early in 1958, he was subjected to sharp criticism, some of it from periodicals that had been his warmest supporters. On November 25, 1957, Eisenhower had suffered a third illness, a mild stroke which caused a temporary impediment in his speech; this time the country's sympathy was mixed with concern about the President's ability to measure up to the demands of his office.

Hawaii became the 50th state on August 21, 1959. The stamp shows eight of some 20 Hawaiian islands (only seven are inhabited) and a native warrior of earlier times. After Mark Twain visited the 1,600-mile chain in 1866, he called it "the loveliest fleet of islands that lies anchored in any ocean."

At the same time that Eisenhower was facing a rising tide of criticism of his leadership, his Administration was hurt by scandal. Eisenhower had come to office as the leader of a "crusade" for decency in government. In the 1954 campaign the President had mentioned with pride that "not one appointee of this Administration has been involved in scandal or corruption."

But before long the Administration was rocked by a series of disclosures of conflict-of-interest violations by the President's appointees and charges of influence-peddling by Vice President Nixon's former campaign manager. Before the dust settled, a series of high-placed officials had handed in their resignations: Secretary of the Air Force Harold E. Talbott; the chairman of the Interstate Commerce Commission; the public buildings administrator; the General Services administrator.

Of all the officials of the Administration, the closest to Eisenhower was Assistant to the President Sherman Adams. Callers at the White House commented on how frequently the President told them: "Take it up with Sherman." When critics aired their complaints that Adams had too much power, Eisenhower responded angrily: "The trouble with these people is they don't recognize integrity."

In 1958 a congressional subcommittee came up with some startling revelations. It reported that a Boston textile manufacturer named Bernard Goldfine had paid for a vicuña coat and had picked up hotel bills for Adams, a long-time friend. The presidential assistant, it seemed, had interceded for Goldfine when the manufacturer got into trouble with the Federal Trade Commission and the Securities and Exchange Commission. Adams' transgressions were not of a major kind, but they carried directly into the White House and made a mockery of the Eisenhower "crusade." Since fur coats had been a symbol of the Truman scandals, the episode of the vicuña coat was especially embarrassing.

Eisenhower rebuffed demands that he dismiss his aide. "I need him," the President said. Adams hung on in office until September 22, intensely unpopular with G.O.P. leaders and a target for the gleeful Democrats. At last he resigned, but he had stayed on just long enough to keep the issue alive into the 1958 campaign.

Even before Adams' fall from grace, Republican election prospects had been poor. Late in 1957 the economy had taken its deepest plunge since the war. Layoffs in the auto and steel industries brought an unexpected halt to the "Eisenhower prosperity." Unemployment climbed to 7.7 per cent of the total labor force, the highest rate since 1941.

The Administration, which had taken steps to counter the milder recession of 1953-1954, moved more slowly this time. It forestalled tax cuts and refused to approve substantial pump-priming proposals; the government, Eisenhower explained, was giving "the private citizen and private enterprise a helping hand—not a federal wheelchair." The economy did not straighten itself out until a good deal of potential output had been lost. Even when industrial recovery was achieved, unemployment remained stubbornly high. In November, as the country went to the polls, nearly four million Americans were out of work. In the farm belt, where grain prices had been falling through the Eisenhower years, Benson's policies were more unpopular than ever.

In the last two weeks of the fall's congressional election campaign, Eisenhower attempted to rally his party, declaring that the country faced a choice between "left-wing government or sensible government." But the country sent the Republicans down to a thunderous defeat. The Democrats widened their margin in the Senate from a narrow 49-47 to a stunning 62-34. Their 282-153 House majority was the greatest since F.D.R.'s landslide in 1936.

Three weeks after the elections, Alaska added its first two senators and its lone representative to the Democratic holdings. Officially admitted to the Union as the 49th state on January 3, 1959, Alaska had an area more than twice that of Texas and a population smaller than the least populous state, Nevada. In August 1959 Hawaii joined the Union as the 50th state and sent

By the spring of 1958 the country was deep in a serious recession. Cartoons like this one captured the mood of many Americans. So did wry definitions of the difference between recession and depression. "A recession," went one joke, "is when you lose your job, a depression is when I lose mine."

Nelson Aldrich Rockefeller inherited much from his grandfathers —oil billionaire John D. Rockefeller and potent Senator Nelson Aldrich. After 18 years in appointive posts, Rockefeller decided that only elected officials could make major policy—so he ran for governor in New York and was elected.

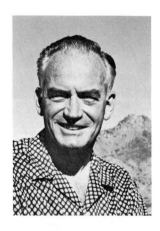

A conservative Republican who won decisively in 1958 was Arizona Senator Barry Goldwater. He flew his own plane around the state and campaigned in slacks and a sports shirt. A personable store owner and Air Force reserve officer, he overcame a two-to-one Democratic lead in registration.

one Republican and one Democrat to the Senate and a single Democrat to the House of Representatives.

For almost six years one of the most popular Presidents in American history had been in office, yet his party found itself in the minority and losing ground with every election. The *Wall Street Journal* asserted: "The responsibility for this disaster, when you come right down to it, must rest on President Eisenhower. It was he who had the sense of direction and lost it; it was he who should have nurtured a party to support his ideas and did not." The President himself was bewildered: "There is a complete reversal; and yet I do not see where there is anything that these people consciously want the Administration to do differently."

The elections shattered the Republican right wing. The "Class of 1946," the conservatives first elected to the 80th Congress, all but vanished. The most notable exception to the trend against the G.O.P. was the victory of the liberal Republican Nelson Rockefeller, elected governor of New York by a half-million-vote margin after a campaign in which he took pains to dissociate himself from the Eisenhower Administration.

AFTER assessing the election returns, the New York *Times* concluded: "Manifestly we are in for a liberal swing. Let us have no doubt of that." Dwight Eisenhower thought otherwise. He now used his influence to turn pending legislation in a conservative direction. A notable example of this was his role in shaping the Labor Reform Act of 1959, a measure which grew out of a Senate investigation of the Teamsters' Brotherhood, the largest union in America. The McClellan committee, with young Robert Kennedy as its counsel, unearthed an appalling pattern of corruption and charged that Teamster President David Beck might have misappropriated $320,000 in union funds. Beck did not stand for re-election, but as his successor the Teamsters chose James Hoffa, who was in equally bad repute with the Senate committee. As a consequence, the Teamsters were ousted from the AFL-CIO.

On the basis of the hearings, Robert Kennedy's elder brother John, the senator from Massachusetts, drafted a bill aimed chiefly at protecting the rights of rank-and-file union members. But with strong backing from the President, Congress amended the measure to add new restrictions on unions. The main effect of the Labor Reform Act of 1959 was to leave strong unions like the Teamsters virtually untouched but to damage weaker unions and impede the spread of unionization in unorganized industries.

At the same time that the President was acting more aggressively in domestic affairs, he was showing a new willingness to take the reins in foreign policy. In April 1959 Dulles resigned; five and a half weeks later he died of cancer. His successor, Christian Herter, was not given an opportunity to dominate foreign-policy making, as Dulles had. With both Dulles and Sherman Adams gone, Eisenhower exercised more personal leadership than ever before.

The world situation confronting the President offered new challenges and new possibilities. On the one hand, the Russians seemed exceptionally truculent. In November 1958 Khrushchev made a new attempt to drive the West out of Berlin; throughout 1959 the fires of the Berlin controversy smoldered. But at the same time the U.S.S.R. showed a new eagerness to reach an agreement with the United States.

In January 1958 the United States and Russia signed an agreement providing for cultural exchange. By the summer of 1959 it sometimes seemed as if everyone in both countries was being exchanged: Nine U.S. governors were touring the Soviet Union, and Soviet First Deputy Premier Frol R. Koslov was visiting America.

While the U.S.S.R. displayed the first big exhibition of Soviet progress in science, industry and culture in the United States since 1939, Vice President Nixon flew to Moscow to open an American exhibition in a Russian park. In Moscow Nixon and Khrushchev got involved in several face-to-face debates, the most famous of them in the model American kitchen at the U.S. exhibit. Although the quarrels revealed Khrushchev's infinite capacity for boorishness, real and feigned, the world was heartened by the fact that leaders of the two countries were at least talking to each other.

In September 1959 the Soviet premier arrived in the United States for a tumultuous 13-day tour. At the outset he displayed bad temper at a Washington press conference, and he behaved with ill grace at Hyde Park, where he was rude to Mrs. Roosevelt. In California he complained at not being permitted to go to Disneyland (police feared for his safety), and when Hollywood arranged for him to see the filming of *Can-Can*, he denounced the dancing as immoral ("a person's face is more beautiful than his backside").

But once Khrushchev reached San Francisco, the mood changed. Both he and his hosts mellowed. Thereafter things moved more cordially. At the end of his visit, the premier spent three agreeable days with Eisenhower at the President's Maryland retreat, Camp David. "Let us have more and more use for the short American word O.K.," the premier urged. After the talks at Camp David, Khrushchev dropped his ultimatum on Berlin, and Eisenhower looked more favorably on a summit meeting. The world began to talk of "the spirit of Camp David" as it once had of the "spirit of Geneva."

In return for the premier's visit, the President made plans to go to Russia in June 1960. Meanwhile he undertook a series of unprecedented trips. In December 1959 he traveled 22,000 miles in 19 days, seeing 11 nations from Spain to India. In February he made a good-will tour of Latin America.

In 1958 Eisenhower had told reporters: "There is no place on this earth to which I would not travel, there is no chore I would not undertake, if I had any faintest hope that by so doing, I would promote the general cause of world peace." As the President made his deeply felt appeal to the people of other lands, much of the world seemed to sense how profoundly he was dedicated to the cause of peace. In India he received a staggering welcome. He was showered with flowers until he stood a foot deep in them, and he was greeted with signs reading: "WELCOME PRINCE OF PEACE."

Eisenhower's reception encouraged new hopes for world peace. As the time for the summit meeting neared, expectations soared higher than at any time since the beginning of the Cold War.

O N May 5, 1960, only 11 days before the scheduled summit meeting, Premier Khrushchev reported to the Supreme Soviet some startling intelligence: Four days before, an American plane had been shot down over Russian territory while on a mission of "aggressive provocation aimed at wrecking the summit conference." The premier did not hold Eisenhower directly to blame, but suggested that "Pentagon militarists" had ordered the flight. Cleverly Khrushchev had baited his trap for the American government.

After Eisenhower's lavish White House reception for Nikita Khrushchev in 1959, the Soviet premier toured America, joking and bubbling proverbs. But in California his good humor turned to anger when he was denied a visit to Disneyland. "Have gangsters taken hold of the place . . .?" he growled.

While Francis Gary Powers, shown with a U-2 model, was in a Russian jail, his father recalled his first flight. "He got out of the plane, told me, 'Left my heart up there and I'm going back to get it.' Well . . . it must be a long way up there . . . he's been up to 100,000 feet and he hasn't brought it back."

135

The American government obligingly walked into it. Perhaps, the National Aeronautics and Space Administration suggested on May 5, the plane was a high-altitude U-2 which, while engaged in weather research over Turkey, had strayed across the border. In any event, the State Department's press officer emphasized on May 6: "There was absolutely no—N-O—no—deliberate attempt to violate Soviet air space, and there never has been."

The very next day the Soviet premier sprang his trap. He now revealed that the Russians had captured the pilot of the U-2, Francis Gary Powers, alive; that he had been shot down 1,200 miles inside the U.S.S.R.; and that he had confessed that he was on a spy mission that had started in Pakistan and was to end in Norway.

Caught in a lie, the State Department now conceded that Powers was on a flight of "surveillance" and that such missions had been undertaken for four years, ever since the U.S.S.R. had rejected the President's "open skies" proposal at Geneva. Yet it indicated that "the authorities" had not sanctioned the flight. Two days later, on May 9, the department reversed itself once more: The President himself had authorized the U-2 program.

O N May 15 the Big Four gathered in Paris amid considerable tension. At their first session on May 16, Khrushchev insisted that if Russia were to participate in the conference, not only must the flights cease, but the United States must apologize for "past acts of aggression" and punish those responsible. Blustering and rude, he accused Eisenhower of "treachery" and a "bandit policy" and suggested that the summit be postponed for six to eight months in the hope that another American President "would understand that there is no other way out than peaceful coexistence. . . ." In a studied insult, the premier withdrew the invitation he had extended to Eisenhower to pay a reciprocal visit to the U.S.S.R.

The President sat through Khrushchev's tirade in a controlled fury, then rejected the premier's ultimatum, although he said the overflights had ended. When the leaders assembled the next day, Khrushchev was not there. The summit meeting, freighted with such high hopes, had been torpedoed.

At an explosive press conference before he left Paris, the Soviet dictator pounded the table, again insulted the United States and warned that any nation which permitted the United States to use it as a base for overflights would be subject to "shattering" blows.

In the dark year of 1960, the U-2 fiasco was only one of a series of disastrous developments which damaged American prestige in many parts of the world: Asia, Africa and, most particularly, Latin America.

Under Truman and Eisenhower, Latin America had largely been neglected unless a threat of Communism was posed. In 1954 the United States intervened to help overturn a pro-Communist regime in Guatemala, but Dulles showed little interest in the massive economic development schemes Latin Americans desired. On occasion the Eisenhower Administration antagonized democratic leaders, as when Eisenhower conferred the Legion of Merit on the dictators of Venezuela and Peru.

In April 1958, after both these dictators had been overthrown, Vice President Nixon set out on a good-will tour of Latin America. In Uruguay he was showered with anti-U.S. pamphlets. In Peru mobs of youthful demonstrators shouted, "Get out, Nixon!" When, against the advice of security officers,

A violent attack on Richard Nixon's car, stalled by jeering, spitting Venezuelan left-wing "students," ended his 1958 mission to South America on a sour note. After his narrow escape, Nixon commented: "If the four men who broke the windows were students, they've been in college more than 20 years."

he drove to the 400-year-old University of San Marcos, students stoned him.

Worse was still to come. In Venezuela the Vice President and his wife were met with howls of hatred and were spat upon. In a working-class suburb of Caracas, Nixon's motorcade was mobbed. The crowd ripped off the American and Venezuelan flags, hurled huge stones which shattered the safety-glass windows and attempted to overturn the Vice President's car.

No longer was there any possibility of Nixon's continuing his tour as scheduled; the only question was whether he could be gotten out of Caracas alive. When it appeared that the Vice President was in danger, Eisenhower ordered paratroopers and Marines flown to U.S. bases in the Caribbean. They were not needed, but it required six truckloads of soldiers to escort Nixon's bulletproof limousines to the airport.

At home Nixon received acclaim for his valor, but the Administration was denounced for so misjudging the state of Latin American opinion as to send the Vice President on a trip where he would be subjected to such indignities. Nixon's tour, wrote Walter Lippmann, was "a diplomatic Pearl Harbor." Few doubted that the Communists had instigated the rioting, but the Communists succeeded only because they were exploiting real grievances. Nixon commented: "The people there are concerned, as they should be, about poverty, misery and disease." The Administration now gave increasing thought to quickening economic progress in Latin America and to encouraging democrats rather than dictators. But some feared that the government's change of heart had come too late.

Events in Cuba suggested that these fears were well founded. On January 1, 1959, rebels under the bearded Fidel Castro overthrew the brutal Batista regime, which had first come to power in 1933. The revolt was greeted warmly in the United States. But within six months Castro had begun to deliver anti-American tirades. He conducted mass trials and executions and established a Communist-leaning dictatorship which snuffed out opposition. With Castro's support, the Soviet Union was able to achieve its first effective penetration of the Western Hemisphere. In February 1960, after a nine-day visit to Cuba, Soviet Deputy Premier Anastas Mikoyan signed an agreement to purchase Cuban sugar and to grant the island a $100 million credit. Castro's successful defiance of the United States served as an exciting stimulant to other rebels throughout Latin America who sought to bring their countries into the Soviet orbit.

As events in Latin America seemed to outrace Washington's policy, the United States took comfort in the fact that there were still nations which seemed firmly in the Western camp. Of these, none was stauncher than Japan, a country whose friendship had been carefully nurtured since 1945. To cement these cordial relations, President Eisenhower planned to visit the island empire. In June 1960 came a shocking rebuff. Following an outbreak of anti-American riots, the Japanese cabinet, in emergency session, decided to ask the President to call off his proposed visit for his own safety. Correspondent Richard H. Rovere wrote from Washington: "If there has ever been a moment of national failure and humiliation comparable to the present one, no one in this dazed capital can identify it."

The unrest in Asia and in Latin America was one phase of the revolution of rising expectations that was shaking the whole globe. On June 30, 1960,

Khrushchev lost his temper often during the fall session of the U.N. in 1960. The translation of his description of one delegate reads: "A jerk and a lackey." His famous shoe-pounding performance is satirized in this newspaper cartoon, captioned: "Is Big Insult, Asking Me To Free MY Colonies!"

The executions that followed Castro's revolution in 1959 led to this Bill Mauldin cartoon. In it the Cuban comforts a doomed man: "Think what could happen to you if we weren't idealists." Mauldin added: "Fidel came out of the hills like Robin Hood and ... began acting like the Sheriff of Nottingham."

in the same month that Eisenhower was barred from Japan and while Cuban-American relations were reaching a crisis, the Belgian Congo celebrated its independence. Within two weeks it was in chaos; tribe turned upon tribe, native upon European. Congolese troops mutinied against their Belgian officers, some fleeing Belgian refugees were dragged from cars and beaten, white women were raped. After an urgent session of the U.N. Security Council, Secretary-General Dag Hammarskjöld (who was later to die in a plane crash in Northern Rhodesia) dispatched an emergency U.N. force, made up of units from Ghana, Tunisia, Morocco and Ethiopia, to restore order.

Two leading 1960 Democratic presidential hopefuls, Senators Hubert Humphrey of Minnesota and Lyndon Johnson of Texas, exchange greetings. Johnson was nominated for Vice President. Humphrey, an ex-pharmacist who visited at least one drug store wherever he campaigned, went back to the Senate.

THE session of the U.N. General Assembly which began in mid-September 1960 was a showcase for the forces of change which marked Eisenhower's last months in office. No longer did the Western world dominate the U.N.; the Afro-Asian nations now constituted the largest voting bloc. At this one session, no fewer than 16 new African countries were admitted to the organization. To Manhattan came leaders of nations either independent of the United States or antagonistic to it—including Khrushchev and Castro. The Communist leaders seemed bent on assaulting not only the dignity of the United Nations but all of the traditions of peaceful negotiation. At one General Assembly meeting, Khrushchev noisily banged his shoe on the table to indicate displeasure; in his turn Castro harangued the Assembly for hours. When, in February 1961, news reached the outside world that the Congolese leader, Patrice Lumumba, had been murdered by his rivals, American Negroes stormed the U.N. Security Council. The violence unleashed at the U.N. revealed a world which seemed to be moving quite out of control, a world in which the United States no longer enjoyed its former pre-eminence.

Puzzled by the fact that the United States seemed to have lost the initiative in world affairs, the country engaged in an intensive self-examination to see if there was something amiss in American society. Most of the introspection came to a common conclusion: that the United States urgently needed a clearer sense of national purpose. More than a year earlier George Kennan had given an address in Washington which aroused widespread comment. "If you ask me," Kennan observed, ". . . whether a country in the state this country is in today: with no highly developed sense of national purpose, with the overwhelming accent of life on personal comfort and amusement, with a dearth of public services and a surfeit of privately sold gadgetry, with a chaotic transportation system, with its great urban areas being gradually disintegrated by the headlong switch to motor transportation, with an educational system where quality has been extensively sacrificed to quantity, and with insufficient social discipline even to keep its major industries functioning without grievous interruptions—if you ask me whether such a country has, over the long run, good chances of competing with a purposeful, serious and disciplined society such as that of the Soviet Union, I must say that the answer is 'no.'"

In 1960 LIFE and the New York *Times* ran a number of articles on the quest for a national purpose, and Eisenhower created a Commission on National Goals to examine the prospects for the next decade. A report issued by the Rockefeller Brothers Fund insisted that it was necessary to define the national purpose in order to win the Cold War and argued that a democracy could "do more than respond to the initiatives taken by its enemies."

Much of the ensuing national debate focused on dissatisfaction with the quality of American life. Many observers argued that the pressures of a bureaucratized society were snuffing out the aspirations of the freewheeling individual, and that the modern American did not seek self-expression but approval through conformity.

The young people who made up the "Silent Generation" of the 1950s seemed to live in a world of shrunken ambitions. They appeared to be obsessed with security; they looked not for worlds to conquer but for a place on the ladder of a corporation or tenure in a university or a civil-service permanency in the government. They showed little interest in public issues; "their minds," complained a professor, "are as quiet as mice."

Not long before the uproar over the deterioration of the national character, one of the nation's best known young people had been the modest, intelligent Charles Van Doren, then an instructor at Columbia, who had a long run as a contestant on the NBC quiz show "Twenty-One." He was snowed under with letters telling him that he, for one, was an idol the younger generation might emulate. Then evidence was made public that the shows, which were ostensibly unrehearsed contests, had in fact been rigged. Testifying before a grand jury, Van Doren denied any part in any crookedness. But a House subcommittee conducted its own investigation—and on November 2, 1959, Van Doren finally admitted he was "involved, deeply involved, in a deception." Nor had he been gradually drawn into the web; he had cheated from the very outset. Disgraced, Van Doren offered his resignation; Columbia immediately accepted.

MUCH of the criticism that emerged from the debate on national purpose was directed at President Eisenhower. The President, it was said, had not only justified political apathy and made indifference to politics respectable, but had failed to meet the crucial issues of the times. "Under the leadership of the President we are promoting private prosperity at the expense of national power," Walter Lippmann protested. "As a result the influence of the United States as a world power is declining." Soviet successes in the space race focused criticism on a consumer-oriented economy which could turn out powerful and ostentatious automobiles but apparently lagged in producing rockets and missiles. "The time has clearly come to be less concerned with the depth of pile on the new broadloom rug or the height of the tailfin on the new car," concluded Senator Styles Bridges of New Hampshire.

The debate over national purpose insinuated itself into the contests for both major party nominations in the 1960 campaign. To avoid a floor fight at the Republican convention, Richard Nixon, leading contender for the G.O.P. nomination, agreed to a platform draft modified to meet the demands of New York's Governor Rockefeller, who had been notably critical of the record of the Eisenhower Administration. Although both the Old Guard and the Eisenhower forces were dismayed by Nixon's willingness to compromise, the Vice President secured the Republican nomination by acclamation.

The contest for the Democratic nomination also revolved around the issue of national purpose. Two of the leading contenders for the presidency, Senator John F. Kennedy of Massachusetts and Senator Lyndon B. Johnson of Texas, had been criticized by Stevensonian Democrats for unwillingness to join issue sharply with Eisenhower's policy of moderation and, some thought, stagnation. They were challenged for the nomination by Minnesota's bold, loquacious Senator Hubert Humphrey.

Long before he became a leading figure in the 1959 television quiz scandals, contestant Charles Van Doren wrote of "the bright little circle of light in which the quiz show contestant basks. . . . All is certainty there." Van Doren himself never knew concern; he was given all the answers in advance.

The busiest schedule of primary campaigning was Kennedy's. But over him hovered the shadow of an earlier campaign: the election of 1928, when, for the first time, a Roman Catholic had made a bid for the White House. Ever since the defeat of Al Smith that year, it had been considered axiomatic that a Catholic could never be elected President. However, historians noted that many who had voted against Smith did so not only because he was a Catholic but also because he represented the threat of the immigrant slumdwellers of the big city. Kennedy was cut from quite different cloth. Although his great-grandfather, Pat Kennedy, had settled in Massachusetts only a century before, the Kennedys had moved upward swiftly; the senator's father had served as ambassador to the Court of St. James's, and his sister had married the Marquess of Hartington. "Jack," said Massachusetts Governor Paul Dever, "is the first Irish Brahmin."

Fighting to overcome the handicap of his religion, Kennedy suffered an ominous setback in the first of his significant primary contests—with Humphrey in Wisconsin. Kennedy did take six of the state's 10 districts, but he lost all four of the heavily Protestant districts. He would have to fight it out with Humphrey all over again—and their next meeting would be in West Virginia, which was 95 per cent Protestant.

In West Virginia Kennedy's managers pulled out all the stops—they exploited the senator's war record, they played crude courthouse politics, they spent money with a lavish hand. Everywhere Kennedy turned he confronted the religious issue, and he boldly met it head-on. "I refuse to believe that I was denied the right to be President on the day I was baptized," Kennedy cried. This turned out to be a shrewd tactic; even West Virginians who admired Humphrey turned to Kennedy to demonstrate that their state was not guilty of intolerance. "You could see them switch," noted a pollster.

On May 10 Kennedy won so decisive a victory in West Virginia that Humphrey withdrew from further competition. That same day Kennedy captured Nebraska. After that, it was all downhill. By convention time Kennedy had such a commanding lead in delegates that all attempts to block him failed. Kennedy was nominated, and at his recommendation Lyndon Johnson was named as his vice presidential candidate.

An exaggerated view of Nixon by the famous British cartoonist Ronald Searle cruelly emphasized the Republican candidate's ski-jump nose. Searle joined the entourages of both parties during the 1960 presidential campaign, reported that "Nixon's nose is an absolute treasure" for caricaturists. Below and on the opposite page are campaign buttons of both candidates.

MANY of those who had been disturbed by the country's apparent lack of national purpose had difficulty working up enthusiasm over either presidential candidate. People wore buttons saying "Neither," and one commentator remarked: "I don't see how either of them can win."

There was a widespread feeling that the political philosophies of both candidates were founded less on principle than on expediency. The commentator Eric Sevareid, arguing that the two men were ambitious opportunists who lacked deep conviction, declared: "The 'managerial revolution' has come to politics, and Nixon and Kennedy are its first completely packaged products. The Processed Politician has finally arrived."

Some observers tempered their criticism of Nixon with sympathy. "Richard M. Nixon," author Theodore H. White wrote, "is a man of major talent—but a man of solitary, uncertain impulse." Suspicious and moody, Nixon was eager to be liked yet slow to give his trust. A prey to self-pity (he told an Ohio audience of how he had never gotten the toy train he had wanted as a child), Nixon gave the appearance, White noted, of being "one of life's losers." On election night, Kennedy would be in his summer home on Cape Cod surrounded by family, while Nixon would await the returns in a California hotel room, a man homeless even in his own state.

Much of the criticism of Kennedy centered on his "coldness." "Behind some of the liberal suspicion of Kennedy," his biographer James MacGregor Burns observed, "is not so much distaste for his views as worry over his temperament." "Let me put it this way," one senator remarked. "If my dear old mother were to fall and break her leg, Hubert Humphrey would cry, but I'm not so sure about Jack." Many liberals also mistrusted him because he had never taken a public stand against McCarthyism despite ample opportunity to do so.

Dᴜʀɪɴɢ the campaign Kennedy, with his boyish good looks and his flashing smile, dispelled some of the impression that he was a man of impersonal detachment; he had even more success in demonstrating that he was a man of deeply held convictions and one who shared the concern over the nation's apparent aimlessness.

But he still had to overcome two great handicaps: prejudice against his religion and the fact that Nixon was better known and believed to be more experienced. Kennedy had hoped to defer the religious issue to the closing weeks of the campaign; this hope was quickly dashed. Early in September a group of Protestant churchmen under the aegis of Norman Vincent Peale, probably the best-known Protestant clergyman in the country, raised doubts about the ability of any Catholic to commit himself fully to the Constitution. Kennedy decided to meet the issue directly. He accepted an invitation from the Greater Houston Ministerial Association to discuss his religious views with them. At Houston he spoke eloquently and directly: "I believe in an America where the separation of Church and State is absolute—where no Catholic prelate would tell the President (should he be a Catholic) how to act, and no Protestant minister would tell his parishioners for whom to vote—where no church or church school is granted any public funds or political preference—and where no man is denied public office merely because his religion differs from the President who might appoint him or the people who might elect him." Before Kennedy concluded, the audience, which had been sullen and suspicious at the outset, broke out into applause.

If the religious issue had not been killed, it at least had been muted. Yet Nixon still led Kennedy at the polls and appeared the probable winner, though by a hairsbreadth. Nixon claimed to be a man of considerably more experience, while Kennedy seemed a stripling who, it was said, was challenging for the White House too soon.

When Nixon agreed to debate Kennedy in a series of national telecasts, the Vice President and his lieutenants were certain that Nixon would enhance his advantage. The Vice President had used the medium to good effect in 1952, and he could now count on a phenomenally large audience. In the 1950s the number of American families who owned television sets had risen from 4.4 million to 40 million, 88 per cent of the nation's families. Millions of Americans—estimates ran as high as 70 million—tuned in to watch the first contest.

The outcome was a major surprise. While Nixon seemed constantly on the defensive, obsessed with scoring debater's points against his rival, Kennedy ignored the Vice President and spoke directly to the nation, enunciating his major theme of national purpose: "I think it's time America started

Caricaturing Kennedy was more difficult, Searle said. "All you have to work with is the hair. It took me the better part of a week before I could get the hang of his face." Here the nominee imbues fund raising with lofty idealism by telling guests: "You are not paying $100 a plate for the privilege of eating . . . you are paying to maintain the freedom of the world."

moving again." While Kennedy appeared calm and self-possessed, Nixon seemed tense and haggard (TV cameras were unkind to his features).

Although three more debates followed, they were largely unilluminating encounters in which various issues were so fuzzed over that neither man's position was distinct; it was the first debate that made its mark and, many thought, determined the outcome of the election. Almost all observers agreed that Kennedy had scored a clear triumph; at the very least, he had demonstrated that he was the equal of the Vice President—no longer would he be dismissed as a callow upstart.

In an election which promised to be so close, both candidates faced a crucial tactical decision: whether to appeal to the Negro voter or to Southern whites. Of all Democratic contenders, Kennedy had been least popular with Negroes before the convention. Nixon, on the other hand, had won favor by his commendable record on civil rights. But during the campaign Nixon lost his advantage by attempting to court both Negro voters and Southern whites at the same time; in the end he failed to poll his full strength with either.

On October 19 Martin Luther King, along with 52 other Negroes, was arrested for taking part in a sit-in in an Atlanta restaurant. The others were released, but King was sentenced to four months' hard labor and spirited away to the state penitentiary. Many doubted that King would emerge from jail alive. Even before King's arrest, some Southern governors had warned Kennedy that if he ever intervened in King's behalf, he could count the South as lost for the Democrats. But Kennedy picked up the phone and called Mrs. King long distance to express his concern. The next morning the candidate's brother Robert telephoned the Georgia judge who had set sentence. On October 27 King was released from prison, alive and well. Nixon, who had had a similar opportunity to act, remained silent.

King's father, a Baptist minister who had opposed Kennedy on religious grounds, announced: "I've got a suitcase of votes, and I'm going to take them to Mr. Kennedy and dump them in his lap." On the Sunday before election, a million pamphlets on the King affair were distributed outside Negro churches. In the election Negro voters gave Kennedy his margin of victory in at least three states, with an electoral count of 55.

On election night the first returns indicated a Kennedy landslide. Connecticut, which had gone for Eisenhower by over 300,000 votes in 1956, went to Kennedy by a wide margin. At 11 p.m. the indicators showed Kennedy already had 241 of the 269 electoral votes he needed. But the last 28 votes came painfully hard. Ohio, where Kennedy had been greeted with frenzied cheering, went to Nixon.

IT was not until dawn that the Kennedy margin seemed ample. At 5:45 a.m., in Washington, the chief of the Secret Service, charged with safeguarding the life of the President-elect, turned away from his television screen, which showed Michigan putting Kennedy over the top. Minutes later 16 agents in Hyannisport, Massachusetts, set out in borrowed cars for the Kennedy home. Kennedy had been elected—but in the tightest race since Harrison won victory by an electoral majority in 1888. Out of a record vote of more than 68 million, Kennedy won by less than 120,000—slightly less than two-tenths of one per cent. A shift of 32,500 votes (4,500 in Illinois, 28,000 in Texas) would have made Nixon the winner.

At the Kennedy inauguration, Robert Frost faltered while reading a special preface to his poem, "The Gift Outright," because he was bothered by the sun's glare. Vice President Johnson tried unsuccessfully to shield the papers. As the assemblage looked on with concern, Frost straightened up and vigorously recited the poem itself, which he knew by heart.

THE GIFT OUTRIGHT

The land was ours before we were the land's.
She was our land more than a hundred years
Before we were her people. She was ours
In Massachusetts, in Virginia,
But we were England's, still colonials,
Possessing what we still were unpossessed by,
Possessed by what we now no more possessed.
Something we were withholding made us weak
Until we found out that it was ourselves
We were withholding from our land of living,
And forthwith found salvation in surrender.
Such as we were we gave ourselves outright
(The deed of gift was many deeds of war)
To the land vaguely realizing westward,
But still unstoried, artless, unenhanced,
Such as she was, such as she will become.

Still Kennedy had won a remarkable victory. He had overcome the handicap of his religion, his "inexperience" and his "immaturity" to defeat the candidate backed by America's most popular hero of the generation.

But at the same time that the nation elected Kennedy, it chose a less liberal Congress than that elected in 1958. By adding a handful of seats to the G.O.P. contingent in both houses, it strengthened the conservative coalition and denied the President-elect a secure working majority. The country seemed to be searching for a national identity, but it still did not sense any special urgency that would inspire a massive liberal upsurge.

O N January 20, 1961, John Fitzgerald Kennedy was inaugurated as the 35th President of the United States. The inauguration ceremonies, which took place in a numbing 20-degree cold, demonstrated how far the nation had come in granting minority groups a prominent place in national life. "The Star-Spangled Banner" was sung by Negro contralto Marian Anderson, who once had been denied the use of the concert hall in the building owned by the Daughters of the American Revolution in the nation's capital because of her race. The invocation was delivered by Richard Cardinal Cushing from Kennedy's home city of Boston (before and after the invocation, Kennedy crossed himself).

The new Administration recognized the importance, too, of the intellectual in American public life. One hundred and fifty-six writers, artists and scientists were invited to attend the inauguration. For the ceremonies Robert Frost, America's most renowned contemporary poet, prepared a special dedicatory preface to his poem, "The Gift Outright" *(opposite page)*. Blinded by the glare of the brilliant sun, the 86-year-old poet faltered, then abandoned his manuscript to recite his poem from memory. He made his last line a tribute to the new Administration, changing "would become" to "will become."

At 12:51 Kennedy took the oath of office as leader of 180 million Americans. In his eloquent inaugural address, the new President showed a sharp awareness of the fact that his election marked a new era in American history. Destined to serve only 34 months before his untimely death at the hands of an assassin, the young leader issued a series of stirring challenges whose fulfillment he would never live to see. "Let the word go forth from this time and place, to friend and foe alike," he said, "that the torch has been passed to a new generation of Americans—born in this century, tempered by war, disciplined by a cold and bitter peace, proud of our ancient heritage—and unwilling to witness or permit the slow undoing of those human rights to which this nation has always been committed, and to which we are committed today at home and around the world. . . .

"In the long history of the world, only a few generations have been granted the role of defending freedom in its hour of maximum danger. I do not shrink from this responsibility—I welcome it. I do not believe that any of us would exchange places with any other people or any other generation. The energy, the faith, the devotion which we bring to this endeavor will light our country and all who serve it—and the glow from that fire can truly light the world.

"And so, my fellow Americans: ask not what your country can do for you— ask what you can do for your country.

"My fellow citizens of the world: ask not what America will do for you, but what together we can do for the freedom of man."

Savoring the moment of celebration, John F. Kennedy and his wife Jacqueline attend the main inaugural ball on January 20, 1961. Despite a heavy snowfall that made travel difficult, thousands of guests gathered at five separate Washington balls to cheer the new President. Each ball was so crowded—12,000 attended the armory affair shown above—that many guests never got to dance at all.

HEAVY WITH HARVEST, a California vineyard yields its grapes to the deft hands of crop pickers. Great improvements in machinery, more use of chemical fertilizers and reclamation of many arid areas (like that seen in background) by irrigation have produced crops unparalleled in 20th Century America.

IMBUED WITH HOPE, some 200,000 Negro and white Americans mass before the Lincoln Memorial to hear speeches on civil rights and Negro aspirations during the 1963 March on Washington for Jobs and Freedom. This demonstration, said Martin Luther King Jr., "subpoenaed the conscience of a nation."

"When our future becomes our history"

The 12 volumes of "The LIFE History of the United States" have chronicled events from the prehistoric era to the 1960s. In his introduction to Volume I, Consulting Editor Henry F. Graff offered a prologue to this "heroic segment of time." Now, in an epilogue that begins on this page, Dr. Graff considers the special meanings which Americans may find in the absorbing story of their past. The pictures that accompany his text were taken especially for this volume by Cornell Capa.

THESE volumes end, as histories should, just before the present begins. Exactly where that point occurs is hard to define precisely. But when the historian finds that the incidents he is recounting are too fresh to be viewed in perspective, he knows he is at the end of his labors. For above all else he must avoid falling into the trap of becoming a chronicler of current events.

What is the meaning of the remarkable tale which breaks off at this point? And what hint does our past offer about the chapters of America's story that will come next? Devising answers to these queries is a challenge that can never be fully met; it is possible, nevertheless, to arrive at some convincing conclusions.

Most important, our history as a whole contains a promise that our form of government and social order will remain vigorous and adaptable. It is not only that

the Constitution has continued to grow and shape itself to each succeeding generation in truly extraordinary fashion. It is that our society itself has survived revolutions, wars and pestilence without serious threat to its continuity, while remaining free in spirit and ultimately in purpose. Even in times of grave crisis the advancement of freedom has been a national concern. The most serious threat to our experiment in self-government, the Civil War, changed the very character of the nation and the states; yet out of the terrible bloodshed there emerged a broadened base for human liberty. The most shattering blow to our national self-confidence was the Great Depression; yet the attack it stimulated on our habits of thought and action led to a richer application of freedom for all Americans—at the very time when the curse of totalitarianism was falling on much of Europe. The most stunning shock of recent decades to American pride in law and order was the senseless murder of President John F. Kennedy; yet in an era marked by violent transfers of power elsewhere in the world, a mourning people found reassurance in the orderly succession to the presidency by Lyndon B. Johnson.

Two towering figures dominate the long and lonely road leading to such triumphs as these. One of them is George Washington who demonstrated, in lessons as

New community concepts, new ways to the abundant life

penetrating today as ever in the past, that free men can find steel rather than ashes in the fires of defeat and disappointment. His is the standard against which in their darkest moments subsequent leaders have had to measure their own aspirations and accomplishments.

The grave, brooding presence of Lincoln is also a constant companion. It calls us back in every generation to the unfinished business of fulfilling in practice our proudest declaration to the world—"all men are created equal." In a nation generally uncongenial to ideologies or dogmatic political commitments, Lincoln symbolizes a powerful equivalent: a national conscience everlastingly warning against timidity and cowardice.

But Americans have responded not only to the powerful prodding of presidential inspiration and example. Every era has had its Goodyear and its Edison, its muckrakers and its utopian reformers, its P. T. Barnum and its Will Rogers, its Susan B. Anthony and its Eleanor Roosevelt, and a golden multitude of others—all presenting, in common, a dedication to individual self-help through new inventions, or new social concepts, or just new ways of living abundantly.

MODERN PATTERNS of life in America are shown in these pictures of a marina *(left)*, a suburban housing development *(right)* and the spiral interior of New York's Guggenheim Museum *(below)*, designed by Frank Lloyd Wright. The flight from the cities since World War II helped settle one third of the nation in suburbs—often in new communities of houses as depressingly impersonal as the blocks of apartments that were left behind. Leisure, both outdoors and indoors, also had a new look. Boating was only one of many participant sports to boom; by 1962 some 37 million boating enthusiasts took to the water in 7.5 million craft. Culture, too, enjoyed a renaissance. Although its significance can hardly be measured statistically, the figures are nonetheless impressive. In 1962 it was estimated that 14 million adults attended concerts, 13 million took adult education courses and 18 million visited art shows.

Historic visions and dreams into reality

If today we Americans share an affluent life full of marvels that not even the monarchs of old could have imagined, the attainment of these comforts has long been on the national agenda. A vision of the goal could have glittered in Jefferson's mind when he heard of the Louisiana Purchase; it must have captured Grant's imagination when he opened the Centennial Exposition in 1876; it surely was in Henry Ford's thoughts when he ordered the five-dollar wage and the eight-hour day in his plants; it dominated the heads and hearts of the sodbusters on the Plains, the boys—like Mark Twain —who saw the heyday of the riverboats, the girls who slaved in sweatshops and lived in hovels, and the numberless teachers who met their charges in one-room schoolhouses. Their dreams, especially their reveries about ease and comfort and relief from the dolor of endless drudgery, are now the stuff of reality. And much in our present suggests that the wishing itself has helped to make things so.

We learn from our national history, also, that we have been busy at an endless game of leapfrog. We made the railroad come upon the scene before the era of canal building had ended; we moved to give the vote to women when fewer than a third of the men were using the privilege; we were mastering the art of flying, and spending billions on rockets, before we knew how to eradicate poverty.

In the playing of this game we have managed to keep the individual in the forefront of the action. Whether it was Horace Mann exhausting himself for the cause of free public schooling, or Wendell Willkie coming from political nowhere to stand for the presidency, or Peter Stuyvesant defying the English even after his defeat was assured, or Harriet Tubman raising the cry of freedom among her people still in bondage, or a myriad of other Americans discovering an uncommon role to fill, and filling it memorably, our American story has been the collective episodes of identifiable individual contributors, who, if only for a moment, once held the center of the stage.

Our history furnishes us, too, with the indispensable clues for understanding our unique outlook as a people. Because we have been spared, for the most part, the anguish of famine and of military defeat on our own soil, we have looked forward to comparable good fortune in the days ahead, and we have behaved accordingly. History has become for us something like a rail journey to a mountaintop: Occasionally the panorama is interrupted by a dark tunnel—possibly by a war or a depression—but quickly the light streams through the

windows again and the trip continues on its predestined upward path.

To picture any other kind of roadway lying before us we must either ignore the past or suppress our inbred expectation that the ride will continue smooth and straight. Unlike Renaissance Man, who imagined that the Golden Age was to be found in ancient Greece and Rome, or Medieval Man, who placed it in the Garden of

THE DRIVE FOR EDUCATION leads to registration jams like this one at the University of California in Berkeley, where nearly 27,000 students enrolled for the 1963 fall term. More than 3.2

Eden, the 20th Century American still clings to his conviction that the Golden Age still lies ahead—beckoning impatiently at the end of a course we have marked out. Our history, then, reaffirms our belief that success for us is ordained by nature and that the stars which shine upon our land shine more brightly than on any other.

In gazing ahead, we can speculate with some certainty about the vista that will in due time reveal itself. In this

148

process we can be instructed, as Americans were, nearly two centuries ago, by the advice of John Dickinson at the Constitutional Convention: "Experience must be our only guide. Reason may mislead us."

It would seem incredible, first of all, that as we approach the 21st Century, the landmarks of the American story should not continue to embolden all men who visit them. The stubbornness of the little band that settled

million were crowding the country's 2,000 colleges and universities in 1960, as war babies began to come of age; and twice as many were expected there by 1970 as the boom continued.

Jamestown, the doggedness of the Pilgrims who found a haven in the American forest, the bustling energy and soaring phrases of the nation-makers who waged a War for Independence and then constructed and breathed life into a Frame of Government without precedent— these things must forever deflect us from false turns in the road.

Then there are the towering monuments of our con-

gressional history: the War Hawks of 1812, sensing a change in the national direction and riding the new tide to a second war against Britain; the compromisers who found in 1820 the formula for bringing Missouri into the Union, and for saving that Union from possible destruction in 1833, in 1850 and again in 1877. And there are the debates that have set the course for our own days—over imperialism in 1899, over the League of Nations in 1919 and the United Nations in 1945, over the Supreme Court in 1937. These are some of the beacons by which we must guide ourselves in whatever we hope to achieve in the field of representative government.

We have had heroes and heroines to delight and enthrall those yet unborn. There were the Adamses and the Roosevelts; there were Jefferson and Bryan, Clay and Wilson, John Marshall and Oliver Wendell Holmes, Clara Barton and Jane Addams, the canal and railroad builders, the miners and textile workers, the farm and plantation hands and hosts of others. They have left a mark on us that our children—and their children—will also wear long after the present generation is gone.

The villains have been surprisingly few (Benedict Arnold, Aaron Burr, the Copperheads, the Ku-Klux Klan, Albert Fall and relatively few more); looking back, we see that ours is not a history of angels in deadly embrace with devils. All our Presidents, for example, have been decent men—even the least capable of them. We tend to study them not in the order of their accomplishments but in the order of their appearance on the scene, as if they could have been interchangeable. The Civil War which broke the apparent calm of our history brought forth little gloating. Jeff Davis, when the victorious Northerners finished threatening to hang him from a sour apple tree, became an object of pity; Robert E. Lee, after warring against the nation he once swore to defend, acquired intersectional sainthood.

Thus, craving continuity and skirting disruption, we Americans have written our history. At every turn it reflects our deep wish to be connected closely to the past. This desire constitutes another fact we may count on, even when tomorrow has become today. It is of central importance to us, too, because at some mysterious point, history-as-it-happens and history-as-we-write-it become intertwined and each is affected by the other.

There is a special reason why Americans are bound by the past and cannot escape it: On the usual scale of events our history is short. (Set the three and a half centuries since the settling of Virginia against the more than 2,000 years since the founding of Paris or the seven centuries since the beginnings of Oxford University.)

Forward with confidence
—but with nostalgia

ON THE GO, some Americans even take their houses with them *(above)*. In New York, at the John F. Kennedy International Airport *(right)*, passengers hurry through the TWA terminal, a striking contrast to the railroad depots of an era when a four-day train trip was the fastest way to cross the continent.

Furthermore, so much of our history has taken place in the age of the photograph (as these volumes amply testify) that minute details of the American story are known or can be ascertained—and can be documented.

We can walk a lane Benjamin Franklin walked, stand in George Washington's bedroom, read the original Plymouth Colony patent, construct a day-by-day account of Lincoln's life, handle the uniforms of our military giants, obtain the text of every Presidential message to Congress. The effect of such intimacy is, in a sense, to make us contemporaries of all our predecessors. It also makes us Janus-headed, simultaneously gazing backward with nostalgia and forward with confidence.

Our history shows us again and again that our problems have never been so hard to solve as we thought they would be. Nothing at present indicates that future historians, writing about the last third of the 20th Century, will have to say that our good fortune in this respect suddenly deserted us. From the start we have been faced periodically with the problem of population, about which so much concern is expressed today. Always we were in apparent danger of either being short of people or having too many of them. The New Englanders who in the first years of the 19th Century bewailed the westward flow of young people as the "Ohio

Away from the terrible tyranny of human want

fever" found a way a generation later to accommodate themselves to an incoming tide of Irishmen they also bewailed. The "hordes" of immigrants who at the turn of this century seemed on the verge of overwhelming New York proved not to have hindered its growth as the center of American cultural life, but rather to have enhanced it. The bold prediction by a famous editor in 1845 that our population in 1945 would come to 250 or 300 million turned out to be far from the fact. But he, like Calhoun, was concerned about America's future—several decades earlier the Southerner had argued for internal improvements, saying: "In one respect, and in one only, are we materially weak. We occupy a surface prodigiously great in proportion to our numbers."

Automation, which has cast its shadow on the future, has also—although in a different form—already

Swimming pools dot this Los Angeles area—incongruously, only a short drive from the ocean. By 1963, there were nearly 300,000 residential

confronted us. No doubt the factory that Samuel Slater designed in 1789 aroused anxiety that man, particularly working man, would one day be obsolete. Few guessed that the factories and their machines would help bring an end to a far worse tyranny than the dislocation of handicraft workers: the terrible tyranny of human want.

If factories gave impetus to unspeakable evils—such as congested living and deformed childhoods, ethnic and racial tensions, and ghastly conditions of labor—they also offered counterbalancing blessings.

For the first time, and nowhere more noticeably than in America, the age-old scantiness of consumer goods was replaced by a sufficient supply of the necessities of life—and more people shared in them than ever before. For the first time the means were at hand to abolish economic insecurity and bring animation to the lives of

pools in the U.S.—100 times as many as in 1948. Once an exclusive luxury of the rich, the pool is now the hallmark of an affluent society.

Broader goals for minorities, for labor

millions for whom existence had been an unending round of pulseless monotony. Before the attainment of these ends, what person recognized that the very factories which produced vice and delinquency would make the goods—cheap bricks and better sewer pipes, for example—that could help do away with all slums, rural as well as urban? Who recalled that occupational diseases were with us long before industrialization? Or that woman- and child-labor from time immemorial had been necessary for successful farming everywhere? Is it too much to ask whether modern automation may not also reveal a new scene for us all—a scene in which the unfettered opportunity to use our talents will give Americans a key to greater creativeness than even the ancient Greeks displayed?

Already we have been transformed into a leisure-loving people with an appetite for creature comforts. The sense conveyed in the title of the 19th Century evangelical hymn "Work for the Night is Coming" has been replaced by the less elegant but more alluring injunction "Have fun." The time-worn precept "Save for a rainy day" has become "Travel now, pay later." But implicit in this alteration of American life is a dialogue on how best to use the extra hours and easier credit.

The movement to guarantee the civil rights of our citizens regardless of the color of their skin has been moving toward a climactic point. One historian has called this period the New Reconstruction. The problem of race, like that of creed, is as old as the first American colony. The fears of established groups that newcomers will dislodge them have been expressed in every generation. The facts of history prove the contrary—as is clear from the record of the Jews and the Catholics, of the Irish and of the Italians, of the Poles and the Puerto Ricans, and indeed of every minority group, all presaging the likely outcome of the present struggle.

If this latest struggle for equality of opportunity is more intense than earlier ones, it is perhaps because we live in a more intense time. Energies are more swiftly marshaled than ever before. But a powerful principle, long recognized, is being confirmed again: True freedom

MANY CAUSES, from peace to medical care, are championed in the placards carried by Labor Day Parade marchers in New York *(opposite)*. One cause—broadened immigration policies —is echoed by the Statue of Liberty *(right)*, whose inscription still invites the world to "give me . . . your poor, your huddled masses. . . ." After World War II the standard of living of Americans soared to a level never before reached in any land.

New fears and uncertainties born of a new technology

cannot be bestowed; it must be won. And each time another submerged group acquires it, the freedom of all other segments of society is immeasurably strengthened. Is there not more reason to believe that we are on the verge of a notable new epoch in our history rather than that we must face a blank wall of frustration for the long future? To answer "no" would be to argue that our history teaches us nothing whatsoever.

THERE are tides in history, and the most steadily recurring is the tide of war. It is not enough to say that the new weapons of mass destruction are simply the latest tools in a long line of death-dealing instruments that had its origin with the hand ax in some cave 500,000 years ago. The capacity for self-annihilation that our technology now offers mankind differs to an unprecedented extent both in degree and in kind.

THE SPACE AGE, dating from "Sputnik," launched by Russia in 1957, has given the U.S. new paraphernalia for peace and war. Peace plans include a rendezvous between two capsules (simulated at right in a laboratory test) after they have gone into orbit. Defense includes the gleaming Titan II rocket *(above)*, which can propel a nuclear warhead more than 6,000 miles.

Our enemies, who once stood at our borders, receded one by one in the 19th Century—France, Russia, Spain and to a lesser extent England. The oceans across which they retreated were then transformed into protective moats for us in the Americas. Today, what Sir Winston Churchill once called "the lights of a perverted science" have put all our enemies and potential enemies on our frontiers again—even when they are 5,000 miles away.

We are again, to be sure, " 'entangled' with the family of man"—we and they are now on one another's door-steps. The fears and uncertainties we must learn to endure in consequence are new in our generation; they test our standards and our traditions and will continue to test them in ways we cannot possibly predict.

Our current problems at home and abroad frequently prompt the comment that "we live in uncommon, revo-

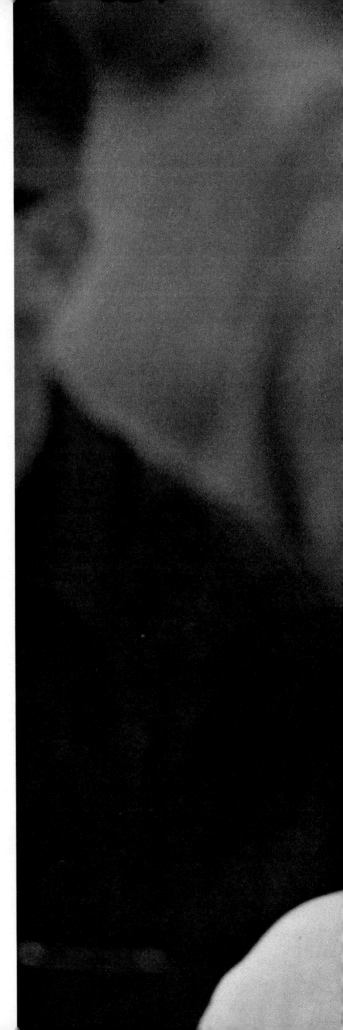

Prepared by experience for a time of revolution

lutionary times." What makes this assertion a cliché is not that it is heard so often at the moment but that it is heard in every era. Was not the attack on Fort Sumter —and the assault on the Constitution it symbolized— the opening cannonade of a revolution? How, if not as a revolutionary step, are we to regard our experiment with imperialism at the beginning of this century—a flagrant violation of our dearest political credo? Did not the coming of steam and the growth of our industries usher in an era of white-hot nationalism and increased production of consumer goods that broke more old molds than any other revolution in man's long history? What shall we say of the spirit of humanitarian reform that, altering the very direction of human development, revealed new and bluer skies for Americans by the 1840s and promises to continue to do so into the indefinite future? Or of that perennial concern for the less privileged of the world that emerges in such open-handed innovations as Point Four and the Peace Corps?

No, we have not fallen on revolutionary days without the experience to face them, and we serve ourselves poorly if we act as though we have. It may be that the act of writing history (and in turn the reading of it) makes the past appear certain and settled, while the future, not yet glimpsed, is formless and threatening. Tremulous people should note that some of the climacterics of our history have resulted from events for which we were ill prepared: the freeing of the slaves, the entrance of America into the First World War, Pearl Harbor or the building of the atomic bomb. The concern over the future should, therefore, never be confused with the burden of it. The burden belongs to posterity.

Toward the historian, time is a neutral. The only assurance we can count on is that its steady flow will sweep in upon us fascinating people and adventures. And when our future becomes our history, we will find it reverberating with alarms and clarions to which we and our children gave heed and found answers. As we weave that story together, some of the threads that now seem to tie era to era will be broken and stretched, and some new ones will be introduced, but the patterns that emerge will be the product still of our tried institutions and the magic of our lofty ideals.

AMBASSADOR OF GOOD WILL, Edward Huiskamp, 26-year-old Peace Corps trainee, reflects the deep vein of generosity and idealism which links America's past with the world's future.

CHRONOLOGY A timetable of American and world events: From 1945

WORLD EVENTS

1945 United Nations organized
1945 Arab League formed
1945 Clement Attlee becomes British prime minister
1945-47 American-British French-Russian Council of Foreign Ministers holds several meetings on peace treaties
1945-49 Nuremberg War Crimes trial
1946 Russians withdraw from Iran
1946 Italy becomes a republic
1946-47 Minor European peace treaties signed
1946-48 Trial of Japanese war leaders
1946-49 Greek Civil War
1947 Palestine partitioned
1947 Russia sets up the Cominform
1947 Soviet control of East Europe consolidated

1948 Years of Ferment Abroad

1948 Israel gains its independence
1948 Communist coup in Czechoslovakia
1948 Benelux customs union goes into effect
1948 Yugoslavia leaves Stalinist camp
1949 North Atlantic Treaty Organization (NATO) set up
1949 Chinese Reds proclaim People's Republic of China
1949 Russia explodes an A-bomb
1949 Indonesia becomes independent
1949 West Germany set up as a Republic
1949 onward Kashmir border disputes between India, Pakistan, Red China
1951 Churchill again becomes British prime minister
1952 Mau Mau terrorism in Kenya
1953 Stalin dies
1953 Riots in East Germany
1953 Mt. Everest conquered
1953 First Chinese Communist Five-Year

POLITICS

1945 Harry Truman becomes President after death of Roosevelt
1945 New York establishes first state antidiscrimination agency
1946 Republicans control Congress for first time in 14 years
1946-48 Strengthening of civil rights provisions in federal and military employment
1947 All U.S. armed forces administration consolidated in Defense Department; James V. Forrestal is its chief
1947 Truman sets loyalty standards for executive employees
1947 Presidential Succession Act puts House speaker and Senate president pro tem next in line after Vice President

1948 Supreme Court rules against racially restrictive covenants
1948 Dixiecrats bolt the Democrats in election campaign
1948 Henry Wallace organizes independent Progressive candidacy
1948 Truman re-elected
1948-50 Alger Hiss case proceeds from hearings to his conviction for perjury
1949 Hoover Commission reports on government reorganization
1950-51 Espionage convictions of Harry Gold and the Rosenbergs
1950-51 Kefauver investigates interstate crime
1950-54 Era of McCarthyism
1951 22nd Amendment limits presidency to two terms
1952 Eisenhower elected President and visits Korea to carry out campaign pledge
1952 Supreme Court bars subversives from teaching in public schools
1953 Tidelands oil controversy ends in favor of coastal states
1953 Puerto Rico given commonwealth status
1953 Department of Health, Education and Welfare established, with Oveta Culp Hobby its secretary
1953 Earl Warren appointed Chief Justice of U.S.

MILITARY and FOREIGN AFFAIRS

1945 Yalta and Potsdam Conferences
1945 Germany dismembered and occupied by the Four Powers
1946 Massive reductions in American armed forces
1946 Termination of Lend-Lease
1946 U.S. proposes international control of atomic weapons and sets up Atomic Energy Commission
1946 United Nations Educational, Scientific and Cultural Organization (UNESCO) founded
1947 "Truman Doctrine" pledges U.S. to protect Greece and Turkey from Communism in Europe
1947 Rio Pact for Western Hemisphere defense
1947 Marshall Plan implements European recovery

1948 Formation of the Organization of American States (OAS)
1948-49 Berlin Airlift
1948-60 U.S. spends $55.2 billion in foreign aid
1949 Point Four plan for economic assistance of underdeveloped nations
1949 U.S. occupation zone of Germany gets civilian high commissioner
1950 Ralph J. Bunche wins Nobel Peace Prize
1950-51 Formation of SHAPE to coordinate European defenses
1950-51 Peace treaties signed with Japan and West Germany
1950-53 Korean War
1951 Truman removes General MacArthur from command
1951-53 Korean truce talks
1952 Development of the B-52 bomber
1952 Australia-New Zealand-U.S. (ANZUS) Pact
1953 Testing of atomic artillery shells
1953 George C. Marshall wins Nobel Peace Prize
1953-54 U.S. negotiates

ECONOMICS

1945-46 End of wartime rationing and price controls on most items
1946 American Federation of Labor readmits United Mine Workers
1946 Office of Economic Stabilization (OES) re-established
1946 Federal government seizes coal mines during a long strike
1946 onward Great expansion of investment companies
1946 onward Appearance of ranch-style and split-level homes
1947 Taft-Hartley Act on labor organizations
1947 Start of "Operation Bootstrap" for Puerto Rico
1947 End of sugar rationing

1948 33⅓ RPM phonograph records first marketed
1948 General Motors signs the first sliding-scale wage contract
1948 Idlewild (later renamed Kennedy) Airport opens — the largest in world
1949 Minimum wage raised from 40 to 75 cents an hour
1949 Walkouts in soft-coal and steel industries
1950 President authorized to stabilize wages and prices
1950 Census shows 150,697,361 inhabitants in continental U.S.
1950 Dedication of Grand Coulee Dam
1951 Employment of women reaches a new peak of 19,308,000
1951 American Telephone and Telegraph becomes first corporation to have more than one million stockholders
1951 onward Rapid growth of the paperback book and long-playing record industries
1952 Ultra-High-Frequency (UHF) channels open to television
1952 U.S. stockholders number more than six million
1953 onward Increased use of automation and computers in industry

SCIENCE

1945 Completion and explosion of first atomic bombs
1946 Radar signals bounced off the moon
1946 Atomic bomb tests at Bikini atoll
1946-50 Atomic elements 96 to 98 identified
1946-52 Development of cortisone
1947 Air Force Captain Charles E. Yeager makes first deliberate supersonic flight
1947 Extensive experiments in cloud seeding produce some rain

1948 First artificial production of the meson, one of the fundamental particles of the atom
1948 Invention of the transistor
1948 Mount Palomar Observatory, with 200-inch telescope, opened
1948-50 Aureomycin and terramycin discovered
1949 Dramamine developed
1949 American Medical Association supports voluntary Medicare plan
1949 Brookhaven Laboratories cosmotron being constructed
1949 First nonstop flight around the world
1951 Completion of microwave relay facilities for first transcontinental television
1952 Presidential commission recommends national health insurance program
1952 12th moon of Jupiter discovered
1952 U.S. announces first successful tests of hydrogen bomb
1952-57 Atomic elements 99 to 102 are produced

CULTURE, RELIGION and SOCIAL EVENTS

1945 Richard Wright's *Black Boy*
1945 Aaron Copland wins Pulitzer Prize in Music for *Appalachian Spring*
1946 *The Age of Jackson*, by Arthur Schlesinger Jr., wins Pulitzer Prize
1946 Canonization of Mother Cabrini, first U.S. citizen so honored
1946 Billy Graham begins evangelistic career
1947 Massachusetts ban lifted on *Forever Amber*
1947 Jackie Robinson is first Negro major league baseball player
1947 Peak year of college enrollment by World War II veterans
1947 Premiere of *A Streetcar Named Desire* by Tennessee Williams
1947 John Gunther's *Inside U.S.A.*

1948 Supreme Court declares religious education in public schools unconstitutional
1948 Norman Mailer's *The Naked and the Dead* and Kinsey's *Sexual Behavior in the Human Male* published
1949 Last encampment of the Grand Army of the Republic
1949 Premiere of Arthur Miller's *Death of a Salesman*
1949 William Faulkner wins Nobel Prize in Literature
1950 *The Lonely Crowd*, by David Riesman and others
1950-52 Construction of Lever House in New York with glass-wall architectural technique
1950 onward Trend towards unity in U.S. Protestant churches
1951 Menotti's *Amahl and the Night Visitors*, first opera produced for television
1951 James Jones's *From Here to Eternity*
1951-52 Supreme Court upholds "released time" for religious education
1952 *T.V. Guide* magazine founded
1952 First appearance of three-dimensional movies
1952 *The Invisible Man*, by Ralph Ellison

1954 ... of Vietnam
1954 onward Chinese Communists bombard offshore islands
1955 Anthony Eden succeeds Churchill as British prime minister
1955 Warsaw Pact formed as a counter to NATO
1955 Argentine dictator Perón overthrown
1955 onward Terrorism on Cyprus
1956 Ghana becomes independent
1956 Revolt in Hungary and unrest in Poland
1956 Egypt nationalizes the Suez Canal
1956 Khrushchev makes "secret" anti-Stalin speech
1956 Tunisia and Morocco gain independence
1956-59 Cuban civil war

1957 Into the Space Age

1957 Harold Macmillan succeeds Eden as British prime minister
1957 Russia launches Sputnik, first man-made satellite
1958 Khrushchev becomes Soviet premier
1958 Algerian rebellion results in De Gaulle's return to power in France
1959 Russian satellite Lunik III orbits moon
1959 Fidel Castro becomes dictator of Cuba
1960 Soviet-Chinese Communist ideological rift begins
1960 onward Riots and anarchy in newly independent Congo
1961 Soviet cosmonaut Yuri Gagarin becomes first man to orbit earth
1961 Dominican dictator Rafael Trujillo assassinated
1961 Communists seal off East Berlin with a wall
1962 Communist China attacks India in Himalayas
1963 French veto British application to join Common Market
1963 Pope John XXIII is succeeded by Paul VI
1963 Ngo Dinh Diem regime ousted in South Vietnam
1964 United Nations sends troops to Cyprus
1964 Prime Minister Nehru of India dies; Lal Bahadur Shastri succeeds him

---

1954 Supreme Court declares "separate but equal" school facilities unconstitutional
1954 Puerto Rican nationalists shoot five Congressmen
1954 Senate condemns McCarthy
1954 White Citizens' Councils organized
1954-55 Dixon-Yates TVA-area power contracts are challenged
1955 First presidential press conference filmed for TV
1955-57 Unsuccessful bid for public power on Snake River in the Northwest
1956 Montgomery bus boycott brings Dr. Martin Luther King Jr. to national prominence
1956 Independent gas producers included under utility rate controls
1956 onward Supreme Court limits states' powers of investigation in search for subversives

1957 Racial riots in Little Rock
1957 Civil Rights Act provides for federal regulation of voting
1958 Democrats gain in congressional elections
1959 Alaska and Hawaii admitted to statehood
1960 John F. Kennedy elected President
1960 Medical Care Bill introduced in Congress, but fails to pass
1960 New Orleans integration crisis
1961 Kennedy establishes the Peace Corps
1961 Ultraconservative John Birch Society becomes public controversy
1961 23rd Amendment gives District of Columbia residents the right to vote in presidential elections
1962 Rioting fails to prevent enrollment of James H. Meredith, the first Negro at University of Mississippi
1962 Democrats win congressional elections
1963 Supreme Court legalizes peaceful sit-in demonstrations
1963 Racial violence in Birmingham, Alabama
1963 John F. Kennedy assassinated; Lyndon B. Johnson becomes President
1964 Supreme Court rules that districts in state legislatures must be "substantially equal" in population
1964 Civil Rights Act goes into effect after lengthy Senate filibuster
1964 Three civil rights workers are murdered in Mississippi; race riots in Harlem and other Northern urban areas

---

1954 U.S.S. Nautilus, first atomic-powered submarine
1954 U.S. signs mutual defense treaty with Nationalist China
1954 Geneva Conference on Indochina
1954 U.S. leads in Southeast Asia Treaty Organization (SEATO) Pact
1954 Air Force Academy established
1955 "Summit Conference" at Geneva
1955 Peace treaty with Austria
1955 U.S. formally ends German occupation
1955 Civil Defense Coordinating Board established
1955 U.S. pledges defense of Formosa and the Pescadores

1957 Eisenhower extends "Truman Doctrine" to the Middle East
1958 Lebanon requests U.S. intervention in civil insurrections
1958 Exchange of atomic information and materials with allies is authorized
1959 B-70 supersonic bomber program cut back
1959 Eisenhower makes a good-will tour of 11 nations in Europe, Middle East and Asia
1959 Atomic submarines equipped with Polaris missiles
1960 U-2 shot down over Russia
1961 America ends diplomatic relations with Cuba
1961 Kennedy proposes Alliance for Progress to raise Latin American living standards
1961 Anti-Castro invasion of Cuba at Bay of Pigs is crushed
1962 Russia returns U-2 pilot Francis Gary Powers in exchange for spy Rudolf Abel
1962 Russian missiles in Cuba withdrawn after firm American stand
1963 Kennedy gets tumultuous welcome in West Berlin
1963 America, Russia and Britain sign nuclear test ban treaty
1963 Washington and Moscow open "hot line" phone connection to reduce risk of accidental war
1964 Riots over display of U.S. flag in Panama Canal Zone

1954 Flexible parity for farm produce established
1954-55 Construction of the St. Lawrence Seaway
1955 American Federation of Labor (AFL) and Congress of Industrial Organizations (CIO) merge
1956 Federal Highway Act provides for vast road-building projects
1956 Soil-Bank Act encourages limited farm-acreage production

1957 Congress investigates labor racketeering
1957 AFL-CIO expel the Teamsters Union for corruption
1957-58 Recession
1958 onward Gold reserves drain from U.S.
1959 Rising popularity of American "compact" cars
1959 Four-month-long steel strike
1960 Census counts 179,323,175 inhabitants, including Alaska and Hawaii
1960 American average per capita income sets a new high of $2,218
1961 Federal budget of $80.9 billion sets peacetime record
1961 Kennedy-backed minimum-wage bill loses in House by one vote
1962 New York Stock Exchange shares lose $20.8 billion in value on May 28; greatest one-day drop since 1929
1962-63 Strikes shut down nine New York City newspapers for 114 days
1963 Kennedy authorizes $250-million wheat sale to Soviet Union
1964 U.S. civilian labor force rises to 72,975,000 while unemployment is above four million
1964 Congress passes tax cuts estimated at $11.5 billion
1964 Severe earthquake damage in Alaska
1964 New York World's Fair opens
1964 President Johnson's war-on-poverty program passes Congress

---

1954 "fall-out" problem widely debated
1955 Salk polio vaccine developed
1955-56 Discovery of the anti-proton and anti-neutron
1955 onward Tranquilizers come into widespread use

1957 Asian Flu epidemic
1957 Synthetic manufacture of amino acids
1957-58 First International Geophysical Year (IGY)
1958 First American artificial satellite is orbited
1958 Commercial jet service begun
1958 International agreement reserves Antarctica for scientific purposes
1959 Development of synthetic penicillin
1959 Explorer VI satellite
1960 Tiros weather satellites
1960 First aerial recovery of satellites
1961 Alan B. Shepard Jr., first American in space, rockets 116.5 miles up during 302-mile trip
1961-62 Exposure of birth-deforming drug thalidomide brings stiffer federal drug act
1962 John E. Glenn Jr. becomes first American to orbit earth
1962 Telstar satellite used for worldwide communication tests
1963 Gordon Cooper Jr. orbits earth 22 times in 34 hours and 20 minutes
1963 Mariner II relays information about the temperature of Venus and other information about the planet
1964 Federal medical panel calls cigarette smoking health hazard
1964 Ranger VII takes close-up photographs of moon

1954 Retirement of Arturo Toscanini
1954 Ernest Hemingway wins Nobel Prize in Literature
1954 Poems 1923-1954, by E. E. Cummings
1954 Inauguration of Newport Jazz Festival
1954 Adoption of codes by comic-book industry
1955 White House Conference on Education
1955 Marian Anderson makes her first Metropolitan Opera appearance
1956 The Organization Man, by W. H. Whyte Jr.
1956 Floyd Patterson wins heavyweight boxing title
1956 Avant-garde "beat" literature, Alan Ginsberg's poem, "Howl"
1956 Grace Metalious' Peyton Place published

1957 Jack Kerouac's On the Road published
1957 Publication of Vance Packard's The Hidden Persuaders
1957 Premiere of Archibald MacLeish's drama, J.B.
1958 United Press absorbs International News Service, becoming UPI
1958 National Defense Education Act
1958 Harry Golden's Only in America published
1958-60 TV quiz program scandals
1960 Large-scale mergers of book firms
1960 Hawaii, by James Michener
1960 Presidential campaign debates are seen for first time on TV
1961 Supreme Court upholds some state and local censorship of motion pictures
1961 America and Russia sign agreement for exchange of scholars
1961 Harper Lee wins Pulitzer Prize for her novel To Kill a Mockingbird
1962 John Steinbeck wins Nobel Prize for Literature
1962-63 Supreme Court outlaws New York school prayer, later rules that no state or locality may require the recitation of the Lord's Prayer or Bible verses in public schools
1963 Samuel Barber wins Pulitzer Prize for Piano Concerto No. 1
1964 National Book Award for Poetry won by John Crowe Ransom

FOR FURTHER READING

These books were selected for their interest and authority in the preparation
of this volume, and for their usefulness to readers seeking additional information on specific points.
An asterisk (*) marks works available in both hard-cover and paperback editions.

GENERAL READING

*Agar, Herbert, *The Price of Power*. University of Chicago Press, 1957.

Chambers, Whittaker, *Witness*. Random House, 1952.

Davids, Jules, *America and the World of Our Time*. Random House, 1960.

Freidel, Frank, *America in the Twentieth Century*. Knopf, 1960.

*Goldman, Eric, *The Crucial Decade*. Random House, 1960.

Graebner, Norman, *The New Isolationism*. Ronald Press, 1956.

Hofstadter, Richard, William Miller and Daniel Aaron, *The American Republic* (Vol. II). Prentice-Hall, 1959.

*Johnson, Walter, *1600 Pennsylvania Avenue*. Little, Brown, 1960.

Link, Arthur S., and William Catton, *The American Epoch*. Knopf, 1963.

Moos, Malcolm, *The Republicans*. Random House, 1956.

Morison, Samuel E., and Henry S. Commager, *The Growth of the American Republic* (Vol. II). Oxford University Press, 1962.

Roseboom, Eugene, *A History of Presidential Elections*. Macmillan, 1957.

Truman, Harry S., *Memoirs* (2 vols.). Doubleday, 1955-1956.

COLD WAR (CHAPTER 1)

Byrnes, James F., *All in One Lifetime*. Harper & Row, 1958.

Clay, Lucius, *Decision in Germany*. Doubleday, 1950.

Daniels, Jonathan, *A Man of Independence*. Lippincott, 1950.

Davison, W. P., *Berlin Blockade*. Princeton University Press, 1958.

Ferrell, Robert, *American Diplomacy*. W. W. Norton, 1959.

Mann, Martin, *Revolution in Electricity*. Viking, 1962.

Rapport, Samuel, and Helen Wright, *Great Adventures in Medicine*. Dial Press, 1961.

Solomon, Louis, *Telstar*. McGraw-Hill, 1962.

*Spanier, John, *American Foreign Policy since World War II*. Pall Mall Press, 1962.

White, Theodore H., *Fire in the Ashes*. Sloan, 1953.

THE FAIR DEAL (CHAPTER 2)

Abels, Jules, *Out of the Jaws of Victory*. Holt, Rinehart & Winston, 1959.

Carr, Robert, *The House Committee on Un-American Activities*. Cornell University Press, 1952.

Cooke, Alistair, *Generation on Trial*. Knopf, 1950.

*Lubell, Samuel, *Future of American Politics*. Harper & Row, 1952.

McNaughton, Frank, and Walter Hehmeyer, *Harry Truman, President*. Whittlesey House, 1948.

Rogge, O. John, *Our Vanishing Civil Liberties*. Gaer Associates, 1949.

*Rovere, Richard, *Senator Joe McCarthy*. Harcourt, Brace & World, 1959.

*Taylor, Telford, *Grand Inquest*. Simon and Schuster, 1955.

AN ERA OF BAD FEELING (CHAPTER 3)

Berger, Carl, *The Korea Knot*. University of Pennsylvania Press, 1957.

Donovan, Robert, *Eisenhower: The Inside Story*. Harper & Row, 1956.

Duncan, David Douglas, *This Is War*. Harper & Row, 1951.

Esposito, Vincent J. (chief ed.), *The West Point Atlas of American Wars* (Vol. II). Praeger, 1959.

Fehrenbach, T., *This Kind of War*. Macmillan, 1953.

Feis, Herbert, *The China Tangle*. Princeton University Press, 1953.

Higgins, Trumbull, *Korea and the Fall of MacArthur*. Oxford University Press, 1960.

Jowitt, William Allen, *The Strange Case of Alger Hiss*. Doubleday, 1953.

*Leckie, Robert, *Conflict*. G. P. Putnam, 1962.

"I LIKE IKE" (CHAPTER 4)

Anderson, Jackson, and F. G. Blumenthal, *The Kefauver Story*. Dial Press, 1956.

Angle, Paul, *The American Reader*. Rand, McNally, 1958.

Costello, William, *The Facts about Nixon*. Viking, 1960.

*Goldman, Eric, *Rendezvous with Destiny*. Knopf, 1952.

Lubell, Samuel, *The Revolt of the Moderates*. Harper & Row, 1956.

Mazo, Earl, *Richard Nixon: A Political and Personal Biography*. Harper & Row, 1959.

McCann, Kevin, *The Man from Abilene*. Doubleday, 1952.

Rorty, James, and Moshe Decter, *McCarthy and the Communists*. Beacon Press, 1954.

Rovere, Richard, and Arthur M. Schlesinger Jr., *The General and the President and the Future of American Foreign Policy*. Farrar, Straus and Young, 1951.

White, William S., *The Taft Story*. Harper & Row, 1954.

EISENHOWER ERA, KENNEDY ELECTION (CHAPTERS 5, 6)

Blum, John, and others, *The National Experience*. Harcourt, Brace & World, 1963.

*Burns, James MacGregor, *John Kennedy, a Political Profile*. Harcourt, Brace & World, 1960.

Childs, Marquis, *Eisenhower: Captive Hero*. Harcourt, Brace & World, 1958.

Donovan, Robert, *Eisenhower: The Inside Story*. Harper & Row, 1956.

Fuller, Helen, *Year of Trial*. Harcourt, Brace & World, 1962.

Ginzberg, Eli, and Hyman Berman, *The American Worker in the 20th Century*. Free Press, 1963.

Hughes, Emmet, *The Ordeal of Power*. Atheneum, 1963.

Kelly, Alfred H., and Winfred A. Harbison, *The American Constitution*. W. W. Norton, 1948.

*Lerner, Max, *America as a Civilization* (Vol. II). Simon and Schuster, 1957.

Pusey, Merlo, *Eisenhower, the President*. Macmillan, 1956.

Schlesinger, Arthur M. Jr., *Kennedy or Nixon: Does it Make Any Difference?* Macmillan, 1960.

Sevareid, Eric (ed.), *Candidates*. Basic Books, 1960.

Wechsler, James A., *Reflections of an Angry Middle-Aged Editor*. Random House, 1960.

*White, Theodore H., *The Making of the President, 1960*. Atheneum, 1961.

Wise, David, and Thomas B. Ross, *The U-2 Affair*. Random House, 1962.

ACKNOWLEDGMENTS

The editors of this volume are particularly indebted to the following persons and institutions for their assistance in the preparation of this book: James P. Shenton, Associate Professor of History, Columbia University, New York City; former President Dwight D. Eisenhower, Gettysburg, Pennsylvania; Dr. Marshall Nason, Cleon Capsas and Ed Heath, Peace Corps, University of New Mexico, Albuquerque; Robert L. Tonsing, Martin Company, Denver, Colorado; Hans H. J. Hoogendoorn, Trans World Airlines, New York City; Robert C. Albrook and Paul Thayer, University of California, Berkeley; Sol Novin, Culver Pictures, Inc., New York City; Carl Stange, Library of Congress, Washington, D.C.; Roberts Jackson, The Bettmann Archive, New York City; Gisela S. Knight, indexer for the entire History series; and Judy Higgins.

The author, for his part, wishes to thank his research assistant, Carol Moodie, for her invaluable help, and to acknowledge his debt to Jean Christie and Daniel Leab for aid in research and to Jean McIntire Leuchtenburg for editorial suggestions.

PICTURE CREDITS

The sources for the illustrations in this book are shown below. Credits for pictures from left to right are separated by semicolons, top to bottom by dashes. Sources have been abbreviated as follows: Brown—Brown Brothers; Culver—Culver Pictures; UPI—United Press International

Cover—Albert Fenn

End papers drawn by Thomas Vroman

CHAPTER 1: 6—Dmitri Kessel. 8, 9—Merritt Ruddick; UPI. 10, 11—TIME covers by Boris Chaliapin except top left TIME cover by Ernest Hamlin Baker. 12, 13—Copyright 1945 Bill Mauldin; Culver—Matt Greene. 14, 15—Culver; "Don't Mind Me—Just Go On Talking"—from *The Herblock Book* (Beacon Press, 1952). 16, 17—Courtesy Public Affairs Press except right TIME cover by Boris Chaliapin. 18—TIME cover by Artzybasheff—TIME cover by Ernest Hamlin Baker. 19—Fitzpatrick, *St. Louis Post-Dispatch*. 20, 21—Courtesy the National Foundation-March of Dimes; U.S. Air Force. 22, 23—Hank Walker; courtesy Hans Passburg, Yankee Atomic Electric Company. 24, 25—Emil Schulthess from Black Star; Fritz Goro; Michael Rougier. 26, 27—Data Systems Division, International Business Machines Corporation; Fritz Goro. 28—Mark Kauffman. 29—Jacques Andre—J. R. Eyerman. 30, 31—Eliot Elisofon.

CHAPTER 2: 32—James Whitmore, courtesy Grand Lodge A.F. and A.M. of Missouri. 34, 35—"You Folks Hear Any Talk About A Housing Shortage?"—from *The Herblock Book* (Beacon Press, 1952); TIME cover by Artzybasheff. 36, 37—UPI; Wide World Photos. 39—TIME cover by Ernest Hamlin Baker. 40, 41—New York Public Library; Brown—Dan Hardy. 42—W. Eugene Smith. 43—TIME covers by Ernest Hamlin Baker except top TIME cover by Artzybasheff. 45—TIME cover by Boris Chaliapin. 46, 47—Howard Sochurek; Hank Walker. 48, 49—James Whitmore except top center Thomas D. McAvoy. 50—Left: UPI; right: Hank Walker; Robert W. Kelley—Hank Walker; UPI. 51—Joe Scherschel. 52, 53—Hank Walker.

CHAPTER 3: 54—Michael Rougier. 56—"You Mean I'm Supposed To Stand On That?"—from *The Herblock Book* (Beacon Press, 1952). 58—TIME cover by Artzybasheff. 59—UPI except bottom. 60, 61—Mark Kauffman; U.S. Army. 62—"Those Are The Flags Of Various Gangster Mobs And Millionaires. Now Shut Up"—from *The Herblock Book* (Beacon Press, 1952). 64, 65—UPI; Joe Scherschel. 66, 67—David Douglas Duncan—U.S. Air Force. 68, 69—Bert Hardy for *Picture Post* from Black Star; Hank Walker. 70—John Dominis—Hank Walker—David Douglas Duncan. 71—David Douglas Duncan. 72, 73—Left: Jun Miki—Harries-Clichy Peterson; right: Michael Rougier. 74, 75—Michael Rougier.

CHAPTER 4: 76—Ralph Morse. 78—TIME cover by Giro. 80—Wide World Photos—Cornell Capa from Magnum. 81—Culver. 82, 83—Culver except bottom right Warshaw Collection of Business Americana. 84, 85—UPI; Frank Scherschel. 86, 87—UPI except right U.S. Air Force. 88, 89—George Skadding except left Al Muto from UPI. 90, 91—Fenno Jacobs from Black Star; Thomas D. McAvoy; UPI. 92, 93—UPI; Ralph Morse; George Skadding. 94—Ralph Crane. 95—George Skadding; Carl Iwasaki—Mark Kauffman. 96, 97—John Bryson; Robert Phillips; John Bryson—Pierre Boulat. 98, 99—Paul Schutzer.—Hank Walker.

CHAPTER 5: 100—Authenticolor by Lavelle-Crandall, courtesy West Point Museum Collections. 103—TIME covers by Artzybasheff. 104, 105—George Skadding; Frank Jurkoski from UPI. 106, 107—TIME cover by Artzybasheff; Culver—"It Never Existed—And I Killed It"—from *Herblock's Here And Now* (Simon & Schuster, 1955). 108, 109—Brown; UPI. 110, 111—Culver; TIME cover by Ernest Hamlin Baker. 112, 113—Don Uhrbrock; Ernst Haas from Magnum. 114, 115—Gordon Parks; Edward Clark—Arthur Shay. 116, 117—Maynard Clark for TIME; Andreas Feininger; Gjon Mili. 118, 119—George Silk; John Dominis—Hank Walker; Ralph Crane. 120—A. Y. Owen. 121—Willenger from Shostal—Ralph Crane. 122, 123—Left: Dick Checani; right: J. R. Eyerman—Cornell Capa from Magnum. 124, 125—Ralph Morse from *We Seven* by The Astronauts Themselves, copyright © 1962 by Simon & Schuster, Inc. Photograph copyright © Time Inc.—Albert Fenn.

CHAPTER 6: 126—Alfred Eisenstaedt. 128, 129—Don Uhrbrock; Wide World Photos. 130, 131—By Frank Williams in *The Detroit Free Press*; UPI. 132—Gimbels Stamp Collection. 133—Bruce Shanks in *Buffalo Evening News*, N.Y. 134, 135—Nina Leen; UPI—Thomas D. McAvoy; UPI. 136—Paul Schutzer. 137—Culver—from the January 14, 1959, *St. Louis Post-Dispatch*, copyright 1961 by Bill Mauldin. 138, 139—Hank Walker; Jack Zwillinger for NBC. 140, 141—Top: Ronald Searle. 142, 143—Paul Schutzer—from *In the Clearing* by Robert Frost. Copyright 1942, © 1962 by Robert Frost. Reprinted by permission of Holt, Rinehart and Winston, Inc. 144 through 159—Cornell Capa from Magnum.
Back cover—Henkin & Kesten

*This symbol in front of a page number indicates a photograph or painting of the subject mentioned.

17, 57, 63; Berlin blockade and airlift, 18, *19, *90-91; Western alliances, 18-19, 63, 90; China policy, 57-58, 59, 107-108; Japanese occupation policy of U.S., 60; "great debate," 63; massive retaliation doctrine, 106; "liberation" policy for Eastern Europe, 106, 110; Southeast Asia, 107; Quemoy and Matsu crises, 107-108, cartoon 110, 132; Dulles' "brinkmanship," 108; summit conferences, 108, 135-136; easing of U.S.-Soviet relations, 108, 134-135; U.S.-Soviet rivalry vis-à-vis smaller nations, 110-111, 127-128, 131-132; Middle East policy, 110-111, 131-132; Suez crisis, 96, *97, 111; Eisenhower Doctrine, 131; Lebanon crisis, 131-132; Berlin crisis of 1958-1959, 134, 135; U-2 incident, 96, 97, 98, 135-136; Latin American relations, 136-137; U.S. losses of prestige (1960), 136-138. *See also* Cold War; Foreign aid; Korean War; Peace promotion efforts; Treaties; United Nations

Foreign aid: to Greece and Turkey, 14-15, 90; to Europe (Marshall aid), 16-17, 90; to China, 57-58; military, 14, 17, 131-132; to underdeveloped nations, 19, *118-119

Foreign Service, McCarthy investigations, 104

Formosa, 60, 61, 107-108, 132

Fort Monmouth, N.J., McCarthy investigations, 104-105

Fourteenth Amendment, 128

France: and occupation of Germany, 11; Marshall aid, 17; in Brussels Pact and NATO, 19; loss of Indochina, 107; in Suez crisis, 96, 111; and Algerian war, 129

Franchise, Negro, 114, 130

Freedom rides, 114, 130

Freeman, Orville, 44

Frost, Robert, *142, 143

Fuchs, Klaus, 46, 58

Fulbright, J. William, 37, 81

Gallup, George, 42, 43

General Motors Corporation, 35, 102

Geneva summit conference (1955), 108

Germany: concentration camps, 11; occupation zones, 11, 17; war crimes trials, 11-12; U.S. occupation policy, 11, 12, 13, 14. *See also* East Germany; West Germany

GI Bill of Rights, 34

Glenn, John H., Jr., *124, 125

Goering, Hermann, 11-12, cartoon 14

Goldfine, Bernard, 133

Goldwater, Barry M., *134

Gomulka, Wladyslaw, 110

Government, federal: dismissal of subversives, 57, 104; Eisenhower's concept of role of, 101, 102, 133. *See also* Federal aid; Federal regulation

Graham, Billy, 116, *117

Great Britain: and occupation of Germany, 11, 12, 17; withdrawal of aid to Greece and Turkey, 14; postwar loans to, 16; in Brussels Pact and NATO, 19; in Middle East, 110-111, 131; in Suez crisis, 96, 111

Greece: aid to, 14-15, 90; Truman statue, *8; in NATO, 19

Gross national product, 1945-1960 increase, 112

Guatemala, 1954 government overthrow, 136

Guggenheim Museum, New York, *146-147

Halleck, Charles, 36

Hammarskjöld, Dag, 138

Harding, Warren G., 8

Harriman, W. Averell, 109

Harrison, Benjamin, 142

Hartley, Fred A., Jr., 39

Hawaii, statehood, *132, 133-134

Hays, Brooks, 129

Health, Education and Welfare, department created, 102

Hébert, F. Edward, *49

Hendrickson, Robert, 59

Herblock cartoons, *15, *34, *56, *62, *82

Herter, Christian A., 134

Hirohito, Emperor, *61

Hiss, Alger, 46, 48, *49, 55, 56, 57, 58, 63

Hitler, Adolf, 11

Ho Chi Minh, 107

Hobby, Oveta Culp, 102

Hodge, Lieutenant General John R., 60

Hoffa, James R., 134

Hollywood, alleged Communist infiltration, 50, 63

Hoover, Herbert, 63, 79

Hopkins, Harry, *10

Housing: shortage, cartoon 34, 127; federal aid, 38, 45; Negro, 114; suburban development, *147

Humphrey, G. M., 102, 103, *105

Humphrey, Hubert H., 44, *138, 139-140

Hungarian uprising, 1956, 110, 129

Hurley, Patrick J., 57

Hydrogen bomb: development of, 58; testing, *21, 108

Iceland, NATO member, 19

Ickes, Harold L., 35

Immigration: areas of origin, chart 38; Displaced Persons Act, 38, 45

Inchon, landing at, 62, map 63, *68-69

Income: farmers', 103, 121; personal, rise of, 112

Income tax, cartoon 106

India, 107, 110

Indochina settlement of 1954, 107

Indonesia, 107

Industry: growth, 109, *113; 1957-1958 recession, 112

Inflation: postwar danger, and price control, 34-35, 36-37; end of control, 38-39; wage and price spiral, 35, 38-39; federal control powers extended, 45

Integration, struggle for, 114, 127, *128, 130; schools, *96, 128-129; Supreme Court decisions, 114, 128

Intellectuals, Kennedy's recognition of, 143

Internal Security Act (1950), 59

International Bank for Reconstruction and Development, 10

International Brotherhood of Teamsters, 134

International Court of Justice, 10

International Geophysical Year (IGY), 24

International Monetary Fund, 10

Internationalism, 9, 19, 55

Investment, postwar private, 34; overseas, 119

Iran: Soviet pressure on, 12, 14; member of Baghdad Pact, 110

Iraq: member of Baghdad Pact, 110, 131; government overthrow (1958), 131

Iron Curtain, 8, 110; origin of term, 12-13

Irrigation, 144

Isolationism: decline, 9; abandoned, 10, 15-19, 55; vestiges of, 17, 55, 61, 80

Israel, 110, 111; and Suez crisis, 96, 111

Italy: Communism in, 17; Marshall aid, 17; in NATO, 19

Ives, Irving, 59

Jackson, Robert, 12

Japan: A-bomb on, *87; U.S. occupation policy, 60; Eisenhower's visit canceled, 137

Jews: Nazi extermination of, 11; limitation of immigration, 38

John XXIII, Pope, 98, *99

Johnson, Lyndon B., 44, *60, *138, 139, 140, *142; succession of presidency, 144; mentioned, 29

Jordan, 131

Jupiter-C missile, 131

Kaesong armistice conference, 73

Kaltenborn, H. V., 42-43

Kasper, John, 128

Kefauver, Estes, 44, 81, cartoon 81, 109-110

Kennan, George, 15-16, *17, 19, 60, 138

Kennedy, Jacqueline Bouvier, *143

Kennedy, John F., 110, *126, 134, cartoon 141, *143; background, 140; presidential candidate, 139-142; elected President, 139-142; inauguration of, *142, 143; assassination of, 144; quoted, 114, 140, 141-142, 143

Kennedy, Robert F., 134, 142

Khrushchev, Nikita, 110, 131, 134-135; 1959 visit to U.S., *98-99, *135; and U-2 incident, 97, 135-136; at 1960 U.N. session, cartoon 137, 138

Killian, James R., Jr., 127, 131

King, Martin Luther, Jr., *112, 114, 130, 142, 144

Kissinger, Henry, 106

Kitt, Eartha, *122

Knowland, William, *95

Korea, pre-1950 history of, 60

Korean War, *54, 55, 60-62, map 63, 64, *65-75, 77-78, map 79, 83, 90, 106-107; casualties, 61, 62, 64, 70, 74, 83; Chinese forces in, 62, 64, 70, *72-73, 77-78, 90; weapons, *65; air warfare and bombing, *66-67; Truman-MacArthur differences, 78-79, 91, 106-107; as election issue, 62, 77, 83, 92, 106; prisoners, 74, *75, 107; armistice talks, *72, 73, 74, 83, 107; armistice, 64, 74, 107

Labor: estranged by Truman, 35-36, 37; Democrats regain support of, 39; postwar legislation, 39, 134; standard of living, 109; agricultural, graph 102, 121. *See also* Strikes; Unemployment; Unions; Wages

Labor Day Parade, New York, *154

Labor Reform Act (1959), 134

La Guardia, Fiorello, 10

Laser beam, 20, *26

Latin America: aid to underdeveloped nations, 19, 137; U.S. relations with, during Truman and Eisenhower Administrations, 19, 136-137; Nixon's tour of, *136, 137

Lattimore, Owen, *50, 59

League of Nations, 10

Lebanon crisis (1958), 131-132

Legislation: McMahon Act, 13; GI Bill of Rights, 34; Employment Act (1946), 34; price control (1946), 36; Displaced Persons Act, 38, 45; Taft-Hartley Act, 39; 81st Congress, 45; Internal Security Act, 59; 1957 civil rights bill, 129-130; Labor Reform Act (1959), 134

Lehman, Herbert H., 10, *13, 132

LeMay, General Curtis, 18

Lend-lease program, 9, 16

Lewis, John L., 35, *36, 39

LIFE, magazine, 42, 138

Life, way of, recent trends, 112, 138, *146-147, *150-153, 155

Lippmann, Walter, 57, 137, 139

Little Rock, Ark., integration fight, *96, 128-129

Lodge, Henry Cabot, 9

Lodge, Henry Cabot, Jr., 80

London Economist, 17

Los Angeles suburb, *152-153

Lubell, Samuel, 132

Lucas, Scott, 63

Lumumba, Patrice, 138

Luxembourg, in Brussels Pact and NATO, 19

MacArthur, General Douglas, 60, *61, 62, 67, 69, 70; and Truman, 62, 78-79, *91, 106-107

McCarthy, Joseph R., 37, 46, 50, 52, *53, 58-59, 63, 83, 104-106

McCarthyism, *46-47, *50, *52-53, 55, cartoon 56, 59, 63, 104-106; protest demonstration, *51; in 1952 campaign, 82

McClellan, John L., *47, 105

McClellan committee, 134

Machine-tool industry, 34

McKay, Douglas, 102

McMahon Act, 13

Magnesium industry, 34

Malenkov, Georgi, cartoon 58

Mao Tse-tung, 57, 131

Mariner II satellite, 29

Marshall, General George C., 14-17, *18, 57, 59, 82

Marshall Plan, 16-17, 90; Soviet cartoons, *16

Martin, Joseph W., 38, 78, 79, *95, *103

Maryland, in 1948 elections, 43

Masaryk, Jan, 17

Massive retaliation doctrine, 106

Matsu. *See* Quemoy and Matsu

Meat prices controversy, 1946, 36-37

Medical advances, *20, 26, *30-31

Medical care, federal aid to, 38, 45

Medina, Harold, 46

Mencken, H. L., 43

Meteorology, 24, 29

Michigan, in 1948 elections, 43

Middle class, growth through shift of occupations, 109

Middle East: Soviet pressure in, 12, 14, 110; problems, and U.S. policy, 110-111, 131-132; Suez crisis, 96, *97, 111; Lebanon crisis, 131-132

Midwest, benefits of St. Lawrence Seaway to, 109

Military security, Western: U.S. slow in recognizing jeopardy to, 10-11, 13; power build-up, 13-14, 19, *156; military aid, 14, 17; Western Europe, 15, 17, 19, 63, 90; defensive perimeter (1950), 60; massive retaliation doctrine, 106; "New Look," 106; Asian defense alliances, 107, 110; missile gap, 127-128, 131

Millikin, Eugene, *95

Missile gap, 127-128, 131

Missiles, ballistic, 127, *131. *See also* Rocketry

Molotov, V. M., 9, 10, 11, 16

Montgomery, Ala., bus boycott, 130

Morgenthau, Henry, Jr., 35

Morse, Wayne, 59

Moss, Annie Lee, *50

Mundt, Karl, *47-49, 58, 83

Murray, Philip, *39

Music, concert attendance, 147

Nagy, Imre, 110

Nashville, Tenn., racial strife, 128

Nasser, Gamal Abdel, 111, 131-132

National character and values, 109; evaluation, 138-139, 144-158; quest for national purpose, 138

National Goals, Commission on, 138

National income, farmers' share, 103

Nationalist China, 60; and Quemoy and Matsu, 107-108, 132

Natural gas price law, vetoed, 45

Nautilus, U.S.S., 23, *108

Nazism, 11

Negroes: in 1948 elections, 43; discrimination against, *40, *114-115, 128-130; advances of, *41, 45, 129-130; situation of, 112, 114; struggle for equality, *112, 114, 127, *128, 130, *145, 155-156; franchise, 114, 130; 1960 vote of, 142; migration to North, 38

Netherlands, the: Marshall aid, 17; in Brussels Pact and NATO, 19

New Deal: popular support, 37-38; postwar counter-revolution, 38-39; revival, 45

New Dealism tied to subversion, in Republican attacks, 56-57, 58

New Hampshire primary of 1952, 80

New Republic, magazine, 40

New Statesman and Nation, 18

New York, in 1948 elections, 43, map 44

New York City: suburbs, 109; Guggenheim Museum, *146-147; Labor Day Parade, *154

New York News, 57

New York Post, 82

New York Times, 36, 42, 98, 129, 134, 138

New Zealand, SEATO member, 107

Newsweek, magazine, 43

Nixon, Richard M., 37, *48, 63, 80, 82-83, cartoon 140; Vice President, 83, *85, 94, 109, 135; visit to Latin America, *136, 137; 1960 presidential candidate, 139, 140-142; quoted, 107; mentioned, 132, 143

North, civil rights struggle in, 114, *115

North Atlantic Treaty Organization (NATO), 19, 63, 90

Norway, NATO member, 19

Nuclear energy: development of, 13, 58, 131; peaceful uses, *23, 108. *See also* Atom bomb; Hydrogen bomb

Nuclear weapons race, 13-14, 58, 106; testing, 13, *21, *60, 108

Nuremberg trials, 11-12, cartoon 14

Oceanography, 24

Office of Price Administration, 35, 36

Office of War Mobilization and Reconversion, 35

Oklahoma, farming, *120

"Open skies" proposal by U.S., 108, 136

Outdoor life, *146, 147, *152-153

Oxnam, G. Bromley, *50

Pakistan: SEATO member, 107; member of Baghdad Pact, 110

Panmunjom, armistice of, 64, 74, 107; negotiations, *72, 73, 74

Paris summit conference (1960), 135-136

MASTER INDEX

For Volumes 1 through 12

Each number in italics indicates an individual volume, 1 through 12, while an asterisk (*) in front of a page number indicates a picture.

CUMULATIVE LIST OF MAPS FOR VOLUMES 1 THROUGH 12

174

PRODUCTION STAFF FOR TIME INCORPORATED

Arthur R. Murphy Jr. (Vice President and Director of Production)
Robert E. Foy, James P. Menton, Caroline Ferri and Robert E. Fraser
Text photocomposed under the direction of Albert J. Dunn and Arthur J. Dunn

Ɪ

Printed by The Safran Printing Company, Detroit, Michigan
Bound by Rand McNally & Company, Hammond, Indiana
Paper by The Mead Corporation, Dayton, Ohio
Cover stock by The Plastic Coating Corporation, Holyoke, Massachusetts

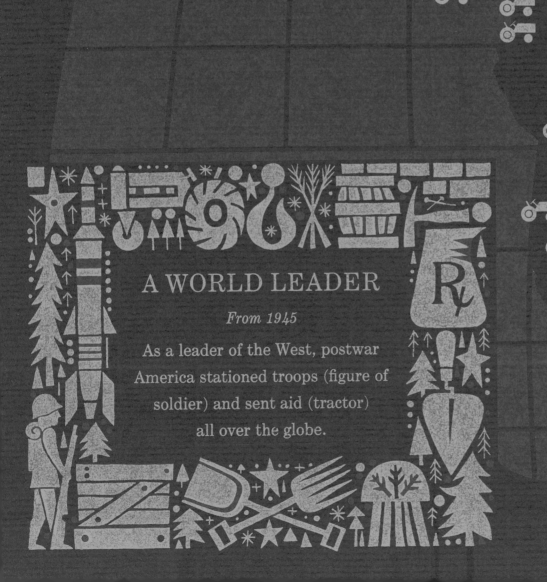

A WORLD LEADER

From 1945

As a leader of the West, postwar
America stationed troops (figure of
soldier) and sent aid (tractor)
all over the globe.